The publisher of this book is generously donating all royalties from the retail sales of **"REMARKABLE RECEPTIONS"** to:

LEMONADE DAY

America was built on the back of small business. Entrepreneurs take risks believing they can realize their dream if they work hard, take responsibility and act as good stewards of their resources. Today's youth share that optimism, but lack the life skills, mentorship and real-world experience necessary to be successful. In 2007, founder Michael Holthouse had a vision to empower today's youth to become tomorrow's entrepreneurs through helping them start, own and operate their very own business...a lemonade stand.

Lemonade Day is a strategic 14-step process that walks youth from a dream to a business plan, while teaching them the same principles required to start any big company. Inspiring kids to work hard and make a profit, they are also taught to spend some, save some and share some by giving back to their community. Since its launch in 2007 in Houston Texas, Lemonade Day has grown from serving 2,700 kids in one city to 1 million children across North America. With the help of partners like Google for Entrepreneurs, Lemonade Day will continue to spark the spirit of entrepreneurship and empower youth to set goals, work hard, and achieve their dreams.

You can learn more about Lemonade Day by visiting:

www.LemonadeDay.org

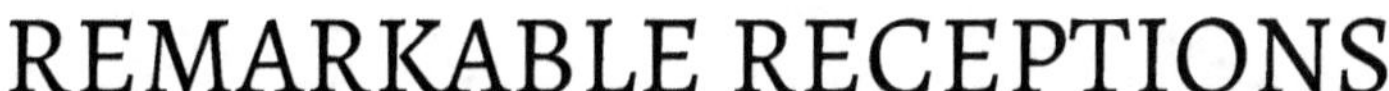

REMARKABLE RECEPTIONS

REMARKABLE RECEPTIONS

Conversations with
Leading Wedding Professionals

VOLUME ONE

By Remarkable Press™

DISCLAIMER AND/OR LEGAL NOTICES: The information presented in this book represents the views of the author as of the date of publication. The author reserves the rights to alter and update their opinions based on new conditions. This book is for informational purposes only.

The author and the publisher do not accept any responsibilities for any liabilities resulting from the use of this information. While every attempt has been made to verify the information provided here, the author and the publisher cannot assume any responsibility for errors, inaccuracies or omissions. Any similarities with people or facts are unintentional.

Copyright © Remarkable Press™

All rights reserved. No part of this publication may be reproduced, distributed or transmitted in any form or by any means, including photocopying, re-cording, or other electronic or mechanical methods, without the prior written, dated and signed permission of the publisher, except in the case of brief quotations embodied in critical reviews and certain other noncommercial uses permitted by copy-right law.

Remarkable Receptions/ Mark Imperial. —1st ed.

ISBN: 978-0-9987085-0-8

CONTENTS

A NOTE TO THE READER

Thank you for buying your copy of **"Remarkable Receptions: Conversations with Leading Wedding Professionals"**. This book was originally created as a series of live interviews, that's why it reads like a series of conversations, rather than a traditional book that talks *at you.*

I wanted you to feel as though the participants and I are talking *with you,* much like a close friend, or relative, and felt that creating the material this way would make it easier for you to grasp the topics and put them to use quickly, rather than wading through hundreds of pages.

So relax, grab a pen and paper, take notes and get ready to learn some problem solving insights for a stress free, perfect wedding day.

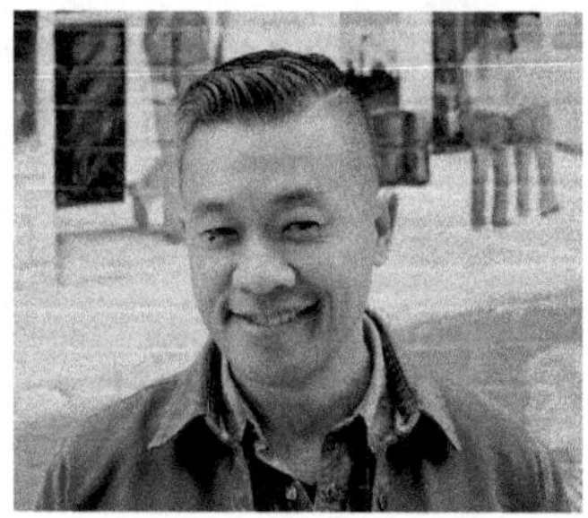

Mark Imperial

Author and Radio Personality

INTRODUCTION

"**Remarkable Receptions: Conversations with Leading Wedding Professionals** is a collaborative book series featuring leading DJ's and Wedding professionals from across the country.

Remarkable Press™ would like to extend a heartfelt thank you to all participants who took the time to submit their chapter and offer their support in becoming 'get the word out ambassadors' for this project.

100% of the royalties from the retail sales of this book will be donated to Lemonade Day. Should you want to make a direct donation, visit their website at: www.LemonadeDay.org

TRAVIS SEIBERT

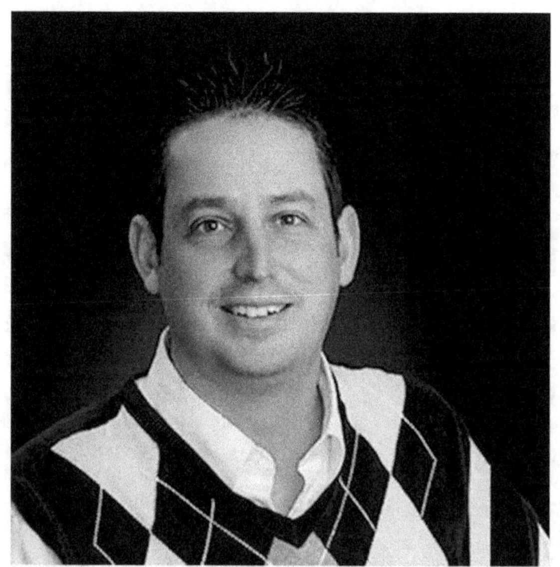

A Conversation with Travis Seibert
Madison Mobile DJ Service

Travis, tell us about your business and the types of clients that you serve?

Yeah, absolutely. I have a very fun, successful business right now that I thoroughly enjoy being a part of. Sometimes businesses are just strictly business. Sometimes it's a lifestyle. For me, this is what I've always wanted to do, what I've always had a passion for and what I've loved. I love getting up every morning and I love helping people.

The business that I have is in Madison, Wisconsin. I'm very lucky to be in this market because it's a thriving city. It's the state capitol, sits on a number of lakes here, two big, huge bodies of water. There's a lot going on here so with the university and the state capitol and Milwaukee and Chicago and Minnesota, as far as Minneapolis and Chicago being all within about 2-3 hours, maybe 4 hours as far as Minneapolis.

It's a great market to be in because I'm able to service a lot of clients. That just means I can take care of more couples and more people on a daily basis which makes me happy at the end of the day because I feel a sense of accomplishment. I work with great clients and, again, I wouldn't want it any other way. I'm in a really good position.

What do you feel is the biggest myth or misconception about the role the DJ entertainer plays in the success of a wedding?

Oh, that's easy. The biggest misconception is that we're just a jukebox -- and that we just hit play -- and that's the furthest thing from the truth. If you have somebody who's passionate about what they do and they want to be as invested as you are in the event then they're going to make the time and they're going to find a way to do that for you.

That means doing the little things. That means showing up before everybody else. That means being the first to arrive and the last to leave. That means doing the little things that make a huge difference like making sure that you're coordinating everything with the caterer, the banquet manager, that you're moving tables and moving chairs, you're holding doors for guests, you're doing all those little small things that nobody ever sees because you're so much more than just a DJ.

Again, nobody ever sees what goes on behind the curtain. They never see the prep that you put in before you even get there. You've got your load in, your load out, getting the stuff into the facility, setting it up, the tear down, there's so many different components that go into that.

When you're actually at the event, you are the eyes and the ears of the client. Nobody wants to supervise their own wedding or their own event. They want to feel like guests at their own party and that's how it should be. That's exactly what we do with Madison Mobile DJ Service is make sure that they don't have to supervise their own event.

We make sure that we keep all that away from them and make sure that by being a good MC and a good DJ, that we communicate really well with the facility manager, with the caterers, with the guests to transition everything throughout the course of the night to make sure that everything's perfect so that they can just live in the moment. I think that is what is vital to the success of an event.

Unfortunately, there's a lot of myths out there and a lot of misconceptions. Don't get me wrong, I'm not picking on young DJs, however, when you're 25 trying to do an event, as opposed to being 40, your focus and maturity are going two different directions.

When you're younger you might be more apt to be more fun and more energetic but you're going to be little bit looser with some of the things or details that you might miss. When you're a little bit older, more mature, you don't let those things slide by because you're more aware of how important they are. Again, there is a misconception out there, anyone can DJ my wedding because I can just plug in my iPod and have something to play music. Then your wedding has no personality, it has no direction, it has nobody there that can guide it to make sure that you don't have to do all that. Having a good DJ, someone that understands all that, is vital to make sure your event is successful.

At the end of the day, you only get one shot at it. Your event is priceless. Having all your friends and family in one place and one time and having them understand the investment that you have in it and making sure that it's everything you want it to be is important because, again, you're probably never going to have that opportunity again.

Unfortunately, you hear or see all the horror stories, maybe on Facebook or on the radio, of weddings or events that turned into, for lack of a better word, a dumpster fire. That's just because, in some ways, there was nobody there to take the lead and to make sure that they were supervising everything or making sure that everything was on point. It's like there was a lack of preparation.

Some might say well I just don't care enough to plan this out or to make sure to have somebody that's there that's invested, that's going to do this for me, that keeps an eye on everything. A lot of those parties are the ones that just say, "We're going to hook up an iPod and we're just going to roll with it." It's just not that simple. Although we believe in the KISS theory, Keep It Simple Stupid, there's just so much more that goes into a wedding or an event or a party or corporate outing or anything like that. You have to be on the same level, as far as the investment that your clients have, otherwise it's just not going to work.

What would you say is the biggest, most common fear your clients have about having a successful wedding day working with an entertainer like yourself?

Two things, one that you won't listen to them. That's number one in our book. Tell me what your expectations are, let me shut up and listen and make sure that we nail that. I think that's the easy part. I think the hard part is exceeding expectations, finding a way to go above and beyond.

If you tell me what you want, if you place an order with me and I was working at a fast food restaurant and you told me what you wanted, that's easy. You told me what you wanted. Now, I've got to figure out a way to go above and beyond and sort of wow you. I think that's vital. That someone maybe didn't understand what their expectations were.

I think number two is that their guests aren't going to have fun, that they aren't going to dance. If you're a good DJ, that's the furthest thing from the truth because your guests have a life of their own or a personality of their own. They're going to come to the party with expectations. They're going to dress up. They're going to look great. They're going to come to the party. They're going to want good food, good drink and they're going to want entertainment. As long as you're able to provide all that, then what happens is the true personality or character of your guests really shine through.

As a DJ, or as an MC, or an entertainer you are the igniter, you are the spark that lights the fire. Once you do that, as a good DJ, then you get the hell out of the way and you let it create itself, the night. You release that energy. You can read magazines, you can read books, you can hear people say don't ever try to control the river because the river will find the way to redirect itself, right?

It's sort of the same thing with that energy over the course of a night. What you do is, you try to channel it a little bit, you get that energy, you get that personality to come to the surface and you let it go and you let it create its own path because, again, each wedding is unique. They're not cookie cutter weddings. The personality of the wedding party and all the guests is what makes the event. We're just there to take that to another level.

What is the biggest or most common mistake that you've ever seen couples make when trying to plan a successful reception that you'd like to make people aware of?

Oh, wow. It's funny that you ask that because I think the weddings that go the best are the weddings where the couples just actually trust the professionals and say, "Look, I know you do this all day every day and twice on Sunday so we trust you," and they let us run with it.

Sometimes what happens is, and I've seen this where you've never done this before, so you've done your research online, or you've read books, or you've taken in information from other people and then you've tried to, and I think this is a strong word so I'm going to caution this when I say this because I don't mean this in any way to be disrespectful and I don't want it to be implied the wrong way, but sort of “micromanage” your event to where you put too much on the plate.

For example, like with timelines, where the expectation is that there's a timeline that's 6 pages long and you expect for everything to be exactly on time. In almost 29 years of doing this, I've never ever seen a ceremony that started precisely on time.

If you were able to get the banquet and the photographer and the DJ and everyone else all on the same page where everything worked on their timelines exactly to the minutes, to the second that they wrote out then that would be an unbelievable feat because it just doesn't happen that way. There's what we call perception and reality. The perception is that you want that $200,000 car. The reality is that you can only afford a $25,000 car.

That's the same thing with a timeline or with a lot of things that happen. It's like, I have these expectations and this is what I envision and this is what actually happens as far as a timeline. Expectations are the killer of dreams. It's not that someone's expectations can't be met. We go above and beyond to make sure that we do that.

For example, what can happen is a photographer will take a bride and a groom and say, "Okay, we're going out to get this shot, then we're going over here." Even if I ask them "Well, how long do you need them?", even if they reply "I need them for 10 minutes," , they can come back 40 minutes later and throw the timeline off.

How do you aDJust to that? A lot of times it's making sure your vendors are aligned and making sure your game plan is well laid out and that everyone has reasonable expectations to make sure your night unfolds the way you want it. As long as everybody works together, there's always a way to do that. I had a wedding recently where the timeline was off by almost an hour and I found a way to get that back on track and that's just by "been there, done that" sort of thing.

Okay, well, we can do this and we can do that so don't worry about this. We'll put this here or we'll do this to make this work. A lot of it is just being flexible in what you do to make sure that you're able to achieve the expectations that your client has.

What inspired you to become a DJ entertainer?

The enjoyment that I see that the couples get at the end of the night. I'm in my early 40's, but I still think I have a hip side or a young side. When I say this hopefully it doesn't come off the wrong way. Everybody has something that they're chasing. I don't do drugs in any way, shape, or form but I'll use this as sort of a metaphor so you can understand it better. It's like chasing that high or that feeling of euphoria that you would get. It's the accomplishment or the feeling of a job well done.

When you have a bride and groom at the end of the night that want to take their picture with you and they want to hug you and they want to tell you how much they appreciate and respect everything you did for them because, again, it's the pinnacle of their life cycle to have all their friends and family and co-workers and everybody say not just a week after the party but a year or 3 or 4 years after the party saying that was the best party I've ever been to in my life is something that they never, ever lose.

When I hear stories about that, I'll run into people who say you did my cousins wedding, it's the best party I've ever been to in my life. That feeling of accomplishment is sort of a high that I can live off of for months.

I stay in contact with a lot of clients that I work with. We become Facebook friends and I'm going to try not to become emotional here, but when I see a couple that I was involved with their wedding, and their reception and their ceremony, when they were just a couple before they became a family.

Seeing brides and grooms that go on to have 2, 3, 4 children and being part of that process makes me emotional.

I can see their children being raised on Facebook, the pictures and I was part of that process. I feel, not only a sense of accomplishment, and I'm not ultra-religious or anything like that, but I do believe in being a good person and I believe the universe works in strange ways.

I always want to be on the positive side. I want to be doing things that are good. I don't ever want to be negative and so I feel like the things that I'm doing in life are very positive so when I'm driving to work or I'm driving back from a gig I don't ever feel like I'm doing something that isn't giving me a sense of accomplishment. I'm happy.

I know some people when they drive to work on a daily basis they hate their life, they hate their job or maybe on the way home, they can't wait to get home. For me, I can't wait to get to my next event because it's a new chapter, it's a new experience and I'm helping somebody create what is the story of their life.

For me, that's why I love doing this and why I have so much passion for it. It just doesn't get better than that. Seeing them in their finest moment, it's just weird, I've always wanted to help other people before I help myself and I firmly believe that if you do that in life that people will find a way eventually to help you get you what you want. I live by that motto.

Can you share a lesson that you learned early on, that still impacts how you perform today?

Yeah, be humble because, again, nobody's perfect. You make mistakes. I thought that I was really good at everything that I do and I am but every once in a while you'll make a mistake. I would make fun of people for making colossal mistakes because I was always so on point with everything.

It's like, I don't want to make a mistake, and I want to make sure that I'm well prepared. It happened at an event where I was on an incredible run. I never had a bad show. I just never have. I've always said if I ever had a bad show it's time to hang it up. I don't probably want to do this anymore because it just means I didn't care enough to be prepared.

I had one wedding I did where, ironically, Jason Mraz has a number of really good songs. He has "I Won't Give Up" and, I'm trying to think of some of the other songs that he had. There's two songs that were very similar to each other. For some reason, it was their first dance song, you pull up your library and there's all the Jason Mraz songs.

I had clicked on the song and loaded it and didn't think anything of it and realized that I actually clicked on the wrong song. They danced to the song and then the groom came over after the very end of the song and he said, "I think you played the wrong Jason Mraz song." The feeling that I had, I felt like you know the top of a roller coaster ride and you go from the apex all the way to the bottom and your stomach falls out. That's the feeling that I had because I had never, ever never done anything close to that, remotely close.

What I learned was, when you make a mistake the first thing that you do is say you're sorry. You own it. The second thing you do is you're humble. You try to figure out a way to make it right.

What I did was I said, "You're right. It's my error. I apologize. I'll figure out a way to correct this." What I did was, we did some more of the formal dancing then I had them come back and I said, I went out with a microphone and I said, "I have to make a confession. I want everybody to repeat after me." This was after the party had been going for a while and everybody was having a great time, but nobody really knew other than the bride and the groom and me that I had screwed up.

I said, "I want everybody to repeat after me. Everybody say, 1,2,3 the DJ sucks." I say, "1,2,3," and they all say, "No, no. We're having a great time. We love you, Travis. No! Why?" "Because I made a huge mistake." The crowds said, "What, what?" I said, "I accidentally played the wrong song for the bride and groom's first dance. What I'd like to do now is bring the bride and groom back out here so that they can celebrate this moment in front of all their friends and family and we do it the right way. Once again, here's the bride and groom." They did the song and everybody cheered and the groom came over and said, "Thank you so much for giving me that moment because that's what I wanted."

They ended up having a phenomenal night. They were very gracious at the end of the night with a gratuity and they wrote me an incredible review. It gave me a very warm, rewarding feeling knowing that even though I made a mistake I was able to rebound from that and they were able to have an incredible experience.

I guess my point is, it was a long roundabout answer, is just be humble. Don't ever think you're better than everyone else. You've always got room for improvement. You can always get better. When you do think that you figured it all out, you realize that you haven't. You can always be better. I'm constantly striving for that. I was just humble there in sharing a story that, again, most people probably wouldn't share just for the fact that if you're not humble enough to let people know that you're now perfect then you're just not real. I'm real and I think my clients know that and I think that's part of the reason why we work so well together is because I always have their best interest in mind. I'm not afraid to put myself out there to make sure that we accomplish that.

How can someone find out more and connect with you?

Oh, easy. I take great pride in our website. Our website is www.madtownDJ.com. I came up with that because they call Madison Madtown. Instead of having Madison Mobile DJ Service and having all that written out, I thought Madtown DJ is easy to remember. Again, I believe in the KISS theory, Keep It Simple Stupid. When I said I take great pride in my website one of the things that's on there is it's very easy to use. It's not overwhelming. You don't have to be a rocket scientist to use it. Everything's laid out in a very easy, very informative way. You can go on there and you can see bios of our DJs. You can go on there and you can get music selection. You can pick your own must-plays, your do-no-plays. There are testimonials on there. There are reviews on there.

I love our website because I think it makes it easy for couples to make a choice on what they want to do as far as their service, but above and beyond, it makes it easy for them to pick their music. There's frequently asked questions on there so they don't have to track me down and say, "Hey, Travis, let me ask you this or let me ask you that." They can go on that FAQ page. Not only did I put the frequently asked questions, I put frequent challenges like, "Hey, this is what we dealt with and this is how we handled it." Things like that.

We try to make it as easy as possible. We have a Facebook page that you can go to as well. We have a Photobooth page. You can always call me as well 608-770-6106. I always answer my phone, or you can reach me via email address which is madisonmobileDJ@yahoo.com.

I'm an old-fashioned guy. I like to talk with people directly over the phone. I know that we're in a day and age now with technology a lot of people just like to text and email. I still like to pick up the phone and call people or have people call me so that I get more of a sense of who they are. That's just me being old-fashioned I guess, in some ways. I do text and email. I do it all.

Our website's really cool because we have a feature on there where you can actually ask questions and we text back and forth. The thing that I like about that is a bride can text me at 10:00, 10:30, 11:00 at night where there's that old, taboo rule where you don't call anybody after 9:00. Things have changed. I answer text messages and emails at any hour. That's one thing that's kind of neat nowadays, you know, wasn't there 15 years ago. That certainly helps as far as connecting with our clients.

SCOTT BARRATT

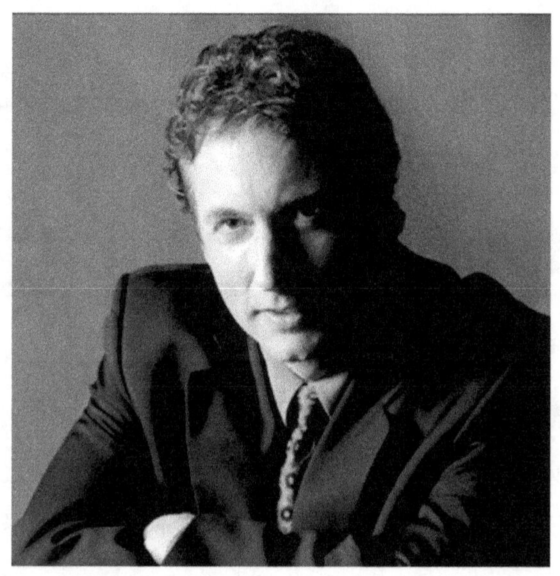

A Conversation with Scott Barratt
of Creative DJ Services

Q: Scott, what inspired you to become a wedding professional?

I was in the radio and TV business. At one point I had 3 national TV shows. I had been fired from almost every radio station in my market. I had lots of experience.

People would come to me all the time. I was working in clubs on the side as a DJ, and say, "Gees I love you on the radio. Can you do my wedding?"

I didn't want to at first, but eventually I relented and realized wow, not only is this a very cool market that I had no awareness of, but also, wow is this ever a market that needs someone who knows what they're doing, because I realized that basically everybody was doing the same thing and they were doing it wrong.

Q: What do you feel are the biggest myths or misconceptions about the role of the DJ entertainer and how it plays into the success of a wedding?

The biggest misconception is that people think a DJ is just there to play the music. In most cases, that is true, because as you well know, most DJs do nothing but sit like a lump in the corner, and then at a prescribed time after dinner, that's their time to stand up and make loud music, which can make or break the last half of the wedding. But looking at that, I thought well why predicate our success on maybe 40% of the duration of the time of the wedding, when we can predicate our success on 100% of the time by entertaining from the word go. I realized, wow, that is a way that we can really affect somebody's wedding to the positive.

Q: What is the most common fear that you hear from brides and grooms when it comes to hiring the entertainer?

Almost every bride and groom that we talk to have been to weddings. They've usually been to weddings of their friends, and sat there and thought, oh god, we want to get married and we're in love. We don't want our wedding to be like this, where they're bored out of their minds at about 9:00pm and thinking how they can slip out the side door without being rude.

They've got a lot of fear, because they want a cool wedding, and they want a wedding that works and has all the dynamics that make a wedding such a special event. Yet, they don't know what to do about it. We found that we're rather unique, at least in our market, because DJs come out and they play the music and they sit in the corner like I talked about.

The wedding planners, which in a movie, usually are very creative people and do lots of cool creative things, well wedding planners that we work with ... And that's not a put down of wedding planners, but they're logistics people.

They've got their clipboards, and are running off a timeline and making sure things work according to that timeline. But in terms of developing a wedding that actually works, in our experience, that's not what they do. Therefore, now you've got a bride and groom. They're in love. I wonder how many weddings they've planned. Well, it's almost always a big fat zero.

Now, they're supposed to be planning their own wedding, yet if something goes wrong with their car, they'll get the diagnostics done from a mechanic. If something goes wrong with their gallbladder, hopefully they'll get a surgeon and not try and take it out themselves. Yet, here they are saddled with the biggest day of their lives, and the success is predicated on them, knowing what to do with a wedding.

Our experience is that because we've seen the way other professionals put it together, nobody has ever really sat back and analyzed it. I find it amazing that there's got to be probably 100,000 people that are in the wedding business, but nobody's ever sat back and thought, okay, it seems like every wedding is the same thing, done the same way, in the same order. Let's analyze it, see if that's the best way to do it.

When I did that a thousand years ago when I started in the business, I thought, you know what, obviously nobody sat back because the order that every wedding goes in is not the most effective order for the entertainment of the guests. It's really especially nowhere near effective or good, or positive for the experience of the bride and groom.

We find that brides and grooms, in fact I've got some celebrity friends who are the Charlie Sheen type. When you're driving to their wedding, you're thinking, Oh my god, what kind of show is he going to put on tonight? You're really actually looking forward to it. But in almost every case, the guy would toe the line and there was no entertainment coming from the groom.

I asked him afterwards, even though I knew what the answer was going to be. I said, "Geesh, what happened there? You were very sedate. I've never seen you like that." It was always the same response, which was, I had my nose to the grindstone all night. I couldn't get my drink on. I couldn't put on a show because I had 200 guests, and I was just trying to give a piece of myself to 200 guests within the 7 hour allotted time. Generally the bride and groom don't have a good experience.

Realizing that, we turned the whole average schedule of the wedding around to make it a lot more effective. You know, a wedding, basically the bride and groom have given apart of themselves to every guest by the halfway mark of the wedding. They've got a picture with every guest by the halfway mark of the wedding. Therefore, they can double their experience, because they got the bride and groom experience of being in a super couple who does things in a unique, crazy efficient way.

Now they've got the last half of the wedding to just be themselves and be a guest at their wedding, and have the party experience, or dance, or whatever they would normally do if they weren't saddled with the responsibility of being a bride and a groom.

Q: How have you been able to help your couples overcome this fear and assure them before it sets in?

I do about a 2 to 3 hour planning session with the bride and groom at the start and show them. You guys have been to weddings. Here's how they usually work. Here's all the things that are wrong with the way everybody does it. Here's a way we suggest.

We don't force anybody of course to do it our way, but we say, here's the way we usually do it, and here are the quantifiable benefits you get from doing it that way. The most common response we get, especially from the brides at the end of this 3 hour meeting is, you know today I was nervous. I was driving here. I booked the venue. I booked you guys. I booked somebody else. But in terms of thinking about that day in the summer when I'm going to get married, I've got the date. I've got the venue and it's all smoke and mirrors. I don't have any details.

But we plan it in chronological order, so basically we're producing a movie of what the day could be. They say, "You know I was afraid when I was driving here today. Now, I wish we were getting married this Saturday, because I've got so much confidence that my wedding is going to be better than any of my friend's weddings."

Basically, that's what everybody wants because they always say I want a wedding that's fun. I want a wedding that's memorable. I want a wedding that's better than my friends. It's been a competition factor in there Mark. We give them that. Then they can't wait for it to happen.

Q: What is the biggest or most common problem that you see at weddings that people should know about so they could avoid?

The most common problem is that people don't sit back, analyze and ask themselves if the order in which we do things work? Does this wedding have the right combination?

You don't want to have it so it's chock a block with events. People don't think about the guest experience from the socio graphics of it. Okay, you're sitting there. Are you going to want to watch something for 5 hours? No, because that's like watching a 5 hour movie. It's too much of a good thing.

What we do is give them that rhythm where we've got little breaks built into it. The smart people in the wedding business know that at the end of dinner, it's almost always a buffet, so people have eaten 5 or 6 times what they would normally eat. The guys all have their belts undone. They're lying around like beached whales in a carb lull, almost falling asleep. They're not ready to party yet.

What we do is make sure we get them out of their chairs immediately, moving around. Then also, the people are smart know that they're not ready to dance. Let's not turn up the music to a high decibel level and aggravate them and keep them from talking. What they don't realize is by giving them that long break after dinner, it's too much nothingness.

What we do is we have a nice undulating wave where it's the dynamics of break and then we always bring their focus back for an event every 15 minutes or so, because you know how it is when you're sitting in a bar. You're talking to somebody. You're engrossed in conversation. You forget you're in that bar.

Just like that if you're at a table and you're having quiet conversation. You forget you're at the wedding. We want to keep them involved all the time, but also give them time to go walk across the room and see their cousins, so they're not stuck in a chair. When they're stuck and sedentary in one place for too long, they lose their energy.

We're always thinking about the energy of the guest and how we can keep it high. That's why another thing that we do is we use something like our kissing dice or trying kissing dice in lieu of the clinking glasses. Well, what we do is we do it right off the start with a presentation that gets a lot of laughs.

Then we control it so it's kind of like a baseball game.

You've got the 7th inning stretch of the baseball game. The reason they have that is that a baseball game is 9 innings. People start, their energy starts to dip, and they're dipping low at 7 innings. They stop the game. Have everybody stand up. Stretch out and sing take me out to the ball game.

Well, we like to do that as maybe a 4th and a 7th inning stretch during the dinner portion, because that's the longest portion of any wedding, where usually the guests are in one place sitting. That way they stand up and they're laughing at somebody who has to perform something because of the kissing dice.

Now they sit down, it's only been a couple minutes they were standing, but they're fresh again. Instead of their energy eroding throughout the dinner portion, when they get to the end of dinner, they're as fresh as we can have them.

As you know, being a former DJ yourself, the thing is you're trying to get those carb loaded people into the mode of getting some drinks into them. Getting them up on the dance floor. We're thinking about that right from the word go of the introduction of the bride and groom at the start of the wedding. That's our objective.

Q: How have couples responded to your unique services?

The clients, they love it. In fact, we're the only company in western Canada. We're in Canada by the way, to win the service excellence award from the Canadian professional DJ association. That's because we are different.

We've been able to cut back on our advertising because of the word of mouth. There are always potential clients, as you know, at every wedding. They see what we do. They say, that's what we got to have. It sure makes it a lot easier when you've got something unique that you can give to people.

Q: What if a couple is very conservative? Can you still help them?

Oh yeah. Absolutely, because the first thing that we do is identify the target. A lot of people just kind of shoot at the imaginary target in their heads, but we realize that every couple is different.

We had one couple, they both play rec league hockey. You can tell I'm in Canada right, talking about hockey? We had 18 of their friends bring their sticks. Hockey sticks. We got them to form an archway of hockey sticks for them to come in under. We did the good old hockey game by stomping Tom

Conners as they came in and had people standing on the chairs stomping.

Then there was another couple where he was in the NHL, but she was quite a famous ballerina. Basically, you get all different types. It's a sliding scale we say, where one is a stuck up downtown wedding on one end, and the other end is a pig roast at the Hell's Angels clubhouse. There's no right or wrong. It's just wherever the client is at.

What we do is identify the vision of the perfect wedding that's in the bride's head. Usually more than the groom, as you know. Once we know where that's at, then we can design it specifically for the mentality of where that bride is at because there's no right or wrong. It's whatever is in her head is what's right.

Q: Scott, how can someone find out more and connect with you?

They can go on the website and find out more about us at www.creativeDJservices.com, send an email to info@creativeDJservices.com, or give us a call at 604-723-6451

SALLY ZITO

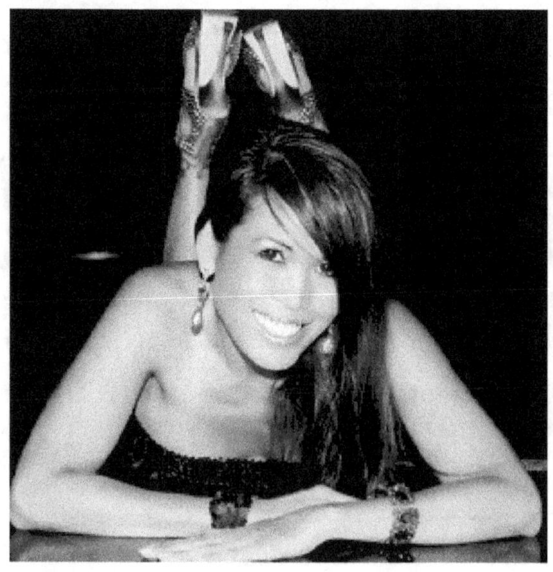

A Conversation with Sally Zito
of DJ Sally Productions

Q: Tell us about DJ Sally Productions and the clients you serve.

After my 21 year career in HR, DJ Sally Productions specializes in weddings, clubs, shows or any occasions bringing unique style of entertainment to many events in several states especially Las Vegas since 2003.

DJ Sally has since entertained many clients and top celebrities at commercials, corporate, clubs, concerts and private events around the world. My clients are very diverse and the genres of music are unique to each event.

Q: What do you feel are the biggest myths or misconceptions about the role your service plays in the success of a wedding?

A DJ/MC plays a key role in the success of a wedding. The best DJ's help you determine the wedding format of your ceremony and reception.

We put together your music needs, take several roles beyond just playing music, making few announcements and crafting high energy entertainment for everyone from the moment you arrive, to your last dance.

Q: What are some of the most common fears people have about having a successful wedding day working with someone in your profession?

The DJ is going to be late or not show up.

Another extreme fear is that you would totally suck.

Does not know what to play and entertain.

Q: What are some of the little known pitfalls that are made when trying to plan a successful wedding day that you would like to make people aware of?

Hiring the cheapest DJ you can find.

Not having a written contract.

Thinking DJ's are all the same.

Not communicating with your DJ.

Not Hiring a DJ right away.

DJ not dressed up professionally.

Q: How have you been able to help your couples overcome these obstacles?

Hire a DJ you like and take the first impression when you meet or spoke on the phone.

Check the DJ's website for background and experience.

Ensure to keep in contact with your professional DJ so that everyone is on the same page and your wedding day will more than likely to be stress-free.

Q: What inspired you to become a wedding professional?

My passion for music. I used to sing at church and I also entertained people with song and dance growing up at school and events. Being a DJ, I am able to express my feelings into it playing music and entertaining.

Q: Can you share a lesson you learned early on, that still impacts how you perform your service today?

Choosing the right music is the most important and most effective way of keeping my customers happy and satisfied. I have learned the importance of reading my crowd and making them comfortable enough to let loose and have a good time!

To this day, it is still the greatest impact of my service.

Q: What's one thing that we may not have covered that you could share with someone who is wanting a successful day?

Always determine what's important and plan ahead of time and cut the unnecessary expenses.

Go over back-up plans with your DJ and make sure the DJ you want is guaranteed to be your DJ.

Let the DJ worry about the timeline.

You only get one chance on your wedding day so keep your DJ informed of your special songs, your plans or any changes to get it right.

Q: How can someone find out more and connect with you?

If you are looking to make your event stress-free and memorable experience. DJ Sally is a skillful Video DJ/MC in any event with a massive library of MP3's and Music Videos. She also has the largest list of Karaoke songs, as well as the technology, equipment and lighting to be self-contained or can simply plug into your sound system.

DJ Sally Productions

Phone: (702) 336-3500

Email: DJsallyproductions@yahoo.com

Website: http://DJsallyproductions.wix.com/DJ-sally-vegas

FB: https://www.facebook.com/DJsallyproductions

ANTHONY COMMISSO

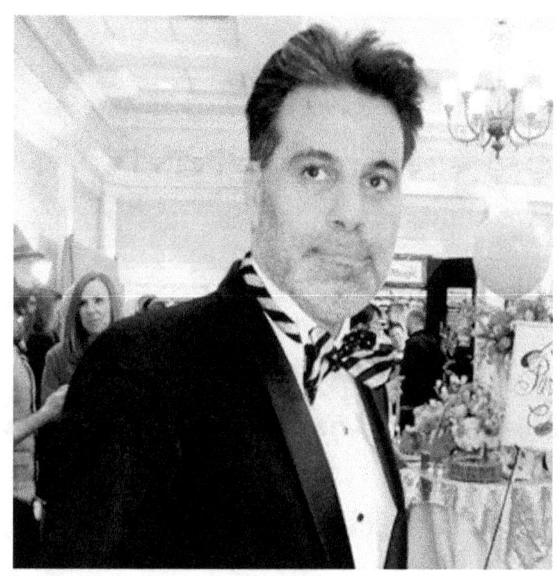

A Conversation with Anthony Commisso
Founder of Tuxego

Q: Anthony, tell us about Tuxego and the types of clients that you serve.

The type of customer that I serve is anyone who is looking to rent formal wear. The primary source of my business of course are weddings, that's the majority. That's the part of the business that I enjoy most.

Q: Anthony, what do you feel is the biggest myth or misconception about tuxedo rental as it plays for a wedding?

That people's expectations are that ... in particular brides ... that they're going to have a disastrous experience. In spite of the fact that they feel extremely comfortable, certainly with me in the very beginning and doing the consultation ... the week of the wedding when my store requires that people come back for a second fitting and we have an opportunity to preview the tuxedo on the client, fine-tune and make any adjustments that by our standards are the appropriate fit.

I think all too often people's expectations are that they're going to get measured the first time, they're going to walk in and they're going to try it on, and they're going to walk out. While that happens in the majority of time, there are those times where we earn our money and where we better serve the client and go the extra step above many others in our industry, especially during that second fitting.

What happens is it's misconceived by the client that making aDJustments, changes, alterations, in spite of the fact that I try to make an indelible impression on the bride and groom when I first meet them, that that is part of our service. That they will sometimes find that as a negative when in fact it's a positive.

There are many other shops, and this is where the industry gets the black eye, our industry more than any other, (and I'll explain why in a moment), is that they will not conduct a second fitting. They'll hand the person the bag.

Even if they conduct a second fitting, if they're within a large window, or large parameter of where the appropriate fit would be, they overlook things and still send them.

It happens the day of because it's something that the bride isn't in control of and doesn't really get to see until everybody is gathered the day of. Then all too often with many other shops it's too late.

Now, is that the majority of occurrences? I certainly think with big box stores ... there are some that just are apathetic to what they do, so if they feel they're close enough and the customer doesn't remark, "Geez, this should be this or this should be that," they don't take the initiative to make the changes and the perception of bride and grooms is that this is an area where things become a disaster.

Now, that said, it is also the part of the industry or the part of the process where they leave setting up the tuxedos and the plans for the guys getting the tuxedos till last, along with the list of multiple professionals they contract to attend to their wedding and all the service and details and making everything perfect.

Then we get them the week of the wedding. The week of the wedding people are typically at their worst, and understandably because they're nervous. Seldom today, is a bride, couple, mother or anyone that isn't nervous about all the details that occur the week of the wedding.

That said, any time there are aDJustments or alterations made I think people also see that as a disaster. Or they see that as a problem. Now in my store I try to convey to the bride and groom that a second fitting is imperative to the success of the wedding because, again, that allows us to make any aDJustments, alterations, and fine-tune it so they're looking their best the day of.

I have a certain very small parameter for how the person is supposed to look in terms of what's acceptable and what's not, and it's a very small window. I want the pants to fall a certain way, I want the jackets to be in a certain place, I want the fit to be a certain way.

In spite of the fact that when we did the initial measurements, and we might have suggested this, or the customer said, “I want tighter, I want looser,” they seemingly forget their preferences and our advice, which occurred way back when they got measured initially, to the time of the second fitting.

Where other shops don't take the time to cover all the details, check the tux's in, really do a good once-over and a good preview of the tux and a good fitting, we go the extra mile and do fine-tune it which people oftentimes find inconvenient.

That's their expectations, or if you will their satisfaction level, can often be lower than that of sometimes being pushed right out the door and never being the wiser that the groomsmen has an ill-fitted tux because sometimes they don't notice. Sometimes it is close enough and that's acceptable to other shops and they just roll with it.

Going forward, we are the only ones that now don't occur the day of. The day of people, the florists, the photographer, makeup artist, all those people that start the day ... the bride has no choice but to roll with it.

Whatever happens, happens, but she's got to adapt to whatever the circumstances are. Whether it's the photographer or officiant doesn't show up, or the photographer somehow has difficulty getting there, makeup artist, whatever that might delay the starting of getting prepared for the wedding ... she has no choice.

The limo is late, whatever other things that can happen, that do happen in weddings, she rolls. By the time they get through the ceremony and then they get to the reception, once they're introduced everything is a party. I always tease my friends that are DJ's that they have it easy. They drop 3 boxes, hit a button, they can fall asleep for 4 and a half hours, 5 hours, and then wake up and everybody is drunk and having a great time.

Q: What have you found to be the most common mistake that couples make when working with a tuxedo shop that you'd like to make people aware of?

That they just make choices based on what they see on Pinterest, or this or that and they don't get candid advice ... that somebody doesn't break down, if you will, the look that they're going for or the look that they're attempting and give them direction as to certain things just don't jive.

A lot of places will rubber stamp whatever a couple picks. You go in the men's clothing stores, there's multiple couples around, there's a couple mannequins, maybe a couple samples at best and a catalog that they're flipping through. They go, "Oh, we saw this, this works for us," and they go with it because they don't do their due diligence and they don't do research to find out who are the people, who are the best places in the area to provide the best quality and the best service.

Fortunately we have won the awards with The Knot, Wedding Wire, we have great reviews. More than anything we are the preferred tux shop of the majority of wedding professionals in this area. I can tell you, five of the most successful DJ's, I'm their go-to guy. Six of the most successful bridal shops, I'm their go-to guy. The largest of venues, banquet catering facilities, I'm their family tux shop. They have no one else, they only come to me.

There are multiple without going down the list of every single profession of every single part of the industry. I have a list of testimonials from professionals that speaks more volume than sometimes other clients, because they say, you're entrusting this person to shoot your wedding for the day and they ask for a recommendation, and that person says, “He's the guy to go to,” that helps a tremendous amount.

I digressed from your question, but really it's to find somebody who is going to give them straight up advice, who is going to take the time with them, who is not going to rubber stamp anything that they pick because there are things that don't go together. Or, let me say this ... there are no rules of yes and no, this works, that doesn't work type of thing ... or cans and cant's, shouldn't, because ultimately it's the brides and grooms.

This is what I tell me couples, “This is your canvas to paint, I serve at your pleasure ... but unlike anywhere else where they're not going to say anything contradictory to your taste at the risk of offending you for fear of losing your business, I am by far the most offensive, obnoxious guy you'll meet in this industry and perhaps in life.

I do so for your own good because I'm going to give you the benefit of my knowledge and my experience. That's what you should be looking for when you're planning the attire for your wedding ... the ultimately, that attire for the gentlemen and the ladies, is the thing that gets captured within the photos that they're going to live with for a lifetime.

Q: Can you share with us an example of a success story, perhaps from one of your most challenging situations?

I think the advice I give sometimes goes beyond just the rent of a formal wear. It goes into the aspect of family dynamics. Sometimes brides aren't sure how to handle who to include and who not to include in the wedding party. Whom to have them walk down the aisle. Whom not to have them walk down the aisle. I will speak upon their life and elicit information.

For example, there will be situations where there will be stepparents and/or the mother or other parent has a significant other. Maybe not married to them, boyfriend, girlfriend, whatever it happens to be. I will tell the person,

"Well, how do you feel about that person? Do you like them? Do you respect them?" If I get a reply that's, "Yes," I say, "Okay. How do you think your mother or father would feel?

"Well, let me say this because we're talking about tuxedos. "Do you like your stepfather? Do you like your mother's boyfriend? Do you respect them?" "Yes." "How do you think your mother would feel about including or excluding this person? Understanding something that, are you also having this person escort your mother when you announce the bridge and groom?"

The parents should be included when doing tuxedos. For example, the father of the bride is the third most photographed person in the wedding.

Provided he's walking her down the aisle, he's doing the father-daughter dance, doing the typical things that the father-of-the-bride does, he's number three because then he's in all the family pictures. You may have some with just the mom and the bride and so forth, but during the day at the beginning of the day, the father is in multiple pictures. Remembering that the bride is the number one photographed person in the wedding, the groom is number two, and, again, the father of the bride is number three.

That said, I believe the father of the bride should be dressed in a tuxedo, not because I'm trying to persuade them to rent more or elicit more in the way of sales, but because I think that is the most appropriate thing when doing formal wear.

Now, going to the other side. Let's say the groom's father, whether the parents are married or not, if they have a close relationship, one in which they're involved in each other's lives, then that father should also ... Let me say, if they're going to have their father ... The groom's going to have his father be included in photos, that would be what I call the "mom and pop shots", where the parents of the bride are standing next to the bride, the parents of the groom are standing next to the groom, then the father of the groom should certainly have a tuxedo because it gives sort of a balance.

I like the fathers to be almost bookends. That's why I tend to strongly suggest and advise that they dress the fathers alike, dress them very simply and tastefully. Less is more because let the mothers shine in their colors. Let the bride shine in their dress. Let the groom stand out by having accessories or tuxedo, however they want to paint this picture, that make him unique to the rest, in particular, the fathers.

One of the things that I'll say to a bride is, when she's wrestling with father over stepfather, "Who's been more involved? Who's the one that helped you with your algebra homework in 10th grade? Who's the one who took you to your cheerleading practice and went and videotaped you at games? Who's the one that took you to colleges and helped you find the appropriate college? Who's the one that gave you advice about boyfriends, relationships, and talked to you about your upcoming wedding?"

Now, that's not to say that that's exclusive one or the other. The father might do some of that just as well, but I always find that there's one person in my experience and in the discussions that I've had with brides and grooms where, and brides in particular, there's been one person far more significantly involved in their life than the other. Say, the stepfather versus the father, or the father versus the stepfather, and depending on who raised them.

This is a really sticky wicket as far as family dynamics and how to handle that. The brides have a lot of trepidation over that and a lot of worry and concern. I've been able to help people make, what I think, is the correct decision in either including everyone or narrowing it down to just one person being the father of the bride. I don't think that makes for the best photos.

In short and in summary, I do get involved in family dynamics. As I was saying, I help the brides overcome the trepidation they have in how to appropriately dress the males in their family. Mother's new husband, mother's boyfriend, father versus stepfather, those sorts of things. That's one of the things where brides are so tremendously thankful for my candid advice. That's something that people won't trend on, I can assure you.

If there are other tux shops, there are very few and far between that would tread those waters in such a delicate situation, but I'm happy to do so because it's all part of painting their picture. It's all part of putting the formal wear together, which again, ultimately is one of those things within the photos that will last for them a lifetime.

Q: Okay. Anthony, what inspired you personally to become a wedding professional and get into the tuxedo industry?

I actually worked initially for the original owner part-time, and we developed a friendship. The opportunity came up because he had multiple locations. He was mismanaging them a lot for personal reasons, and the person who was running his operation essentially, in his stead, or in his inability to stay focused and manage, left the company.

The store that that person was operating ... there had been other stores that he had opened up and other people that he helped get into the business ... I took over what was then a white elephant. That location was just, as other people will tell you, just a bad location. I turned it around, I moved it into a plaza next door. I'm now proud to say I am probably in the top 5% of single owner operated tux shops for volume, and in particular those that work with a wholesale supplier of tuxedos.

If I may, one of the things that is a misconception, if I may go back, is that a lot of shops that carry their own stock try to create fear in the bride and groom that if they don't do their tuxes with a place that actually has everything on premise that they run the risk of errors being made and having problems.

I'm 100% first generation Italian with parents off the boat, so I'm more than qualified to say that that's a lot of those old-time Italian tailor shops that are trying to heighten the fear of brides and grooms.

That also plays into the bride and grooms having some worries about formal wear, when in fact if you find a good tux shop, whether they sub-rent their merchandise, or they have it on the premises, they should be able to handle it in the very same way.

Oftentimes those other shops don't carry multiple sizes in the multiple styles. They have a limited style selection. They have limited sizes. They make you believe that everything is on the premises. Those people have to go and sub-rent to fill in the holes.

The thing is, somebody like me who does 100% sub-renting, I'm at the top of the pecking order. I already have all my merchandise in for next week's weddings and its Thursday of this week. That says something about the value of my business and why my supplier takes such good care of me, that those people won't have the ability to do it.

I'm sorry I reflected back on that, but I didn't want to miss that. Going back to it, I simply got into the business through my friend and persevered and made it a success and just did what I did. I have a tremendous amount of experience with sales background, and I'm a people person. I grew up in the restaurant business, so overcoming objections was something that was easy for me because some people who would come in with a lot of trepidation about preparing, walk out of here and go, "Wow, I never expected it to be that easy. Wow, you made it a fun time. This was great, I didn't expect it to really get this kind of direction. Wow, other places we've gone to were a terrible experience and this was awesome and we're going to tell our friends about you." That only doesn't happen at the consultation that happens on the follow through, once again, as you can see in the reviews.

Q: Can you share a big lesson you learned early on that still impacts how you perform and do business today?

There are multiple things that come to mind. One that I remember is was a father of a bride who came in and got measured. In the old days, we just went off the tape measure and we didn't have people try on merchandise.

What happened is that person said, "No, I'm thinner than that. I'm smaller than that." I said, "Okay, I'll bring you in the other pair of pants. Come back and try them on and see which ones you like and take the ones you like." He didn't come back, they went ahead and I told my associate, just send him with the ones that I knew worked versus the other ones because I didn't want to have an issue.

The customer wasn't satisfied. I still see these people in church to this day, and while it's almost 17 years later, it still feels awkward. Although we'll nod and be polite to one another, it still bothers me because I pride myself on doing a good job.

That was a failure on my part but that also came as a result of the customer's lack of cooperation.

Q: Is there one thing that we may not have covered that you could share with somebody who wants a successful day as it relates to working with a tuxedo shop like yours?

Well one, do your research. Two, ask your other wedding professionals because they'll have booked a venue, they'll have booked a photographer, they'll have booked a DJ, caterer, dresses before.

Get some input from them as to who they know of that is a successful tux shop that they rely on for their own family weddings, for their own client's weddings and friends. That would probably be the first step in moving toward a successful experience with formal wear.

Once again, reiterating the fact that they should work with somebody who is going to sit down with them one-on-one as

I do. I take an hour to an hour and a half with each couple in a very well-presented consultation. I'm not saying there aren't other people out there that do it, I just don't think they do it to the depth that I do.

I think if they take those steps and if they trust in their formal wear provider and they understand the value of what procedures a tux shop has in places, that's what I'd look for.

I'd look for a tux shop that really can nail down, this is what we do. You met with me, this is how it's set up, this is what your guys will do, this is what you can expect, and this is what you should anticipate.

Sometimes they come in a month beforehand and they rush it, sometimes they come in 6 months beforehand. Regardless, when wedding week arrives, their memory isn't as strong as it was at the time we met in the consultation.

Q: Anthony, how can someone find out more and connect with you?

Simply they can go to our website, at www.tuxego.com. They can go to our Facebook page at Tuxego.

Not to be confused with other people, but I actually own the trademark and the dot-com. They can call me at 518-783-0260.

I prefer to talk to people, but in this day and age everybody wants to email. I also on weekends forward my calls to my cellphone so that if there is a wedding occurring, people can reach out to me if they need anything last minute. I also text my grooms two to three hours in advance of their weddings to make sure that they know I'm here and available to them for any reason whatsoever, and to congratulate them as well and let them know that my service didn't stop when they walked out of my store with the tuxedo.

VANESSA HUNDLEY

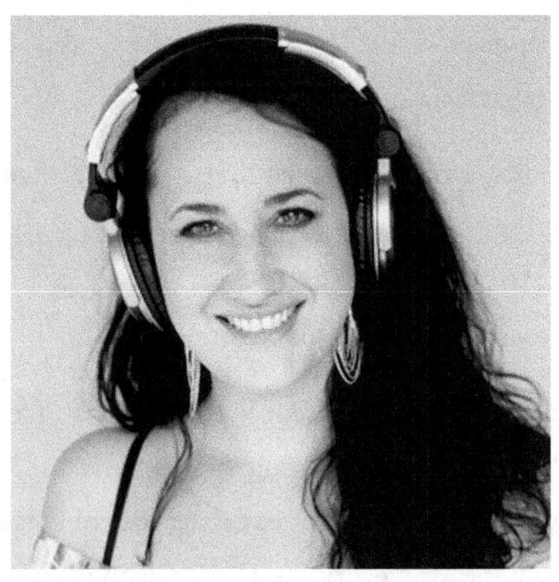

A Conversation with Vanessa Hundley
of Audioprism Entertainment

What makes a really great wedding DJ? Is it the music? Their personality? Or expertise and experience? That is what we will discuss with Vanessa Hundley, the owner of Audioprism Entertainment.

DJ Vanessa Hundley knows that it is a balance of all of these factors. Since her start as a DJ in the vibrant Buckhead/Atlanta party district she has been on a journey of exploring music in all its forms.

She has learned how to use it to create any atmosphere her clients' desire. She draws upon her extensive background with crowds, events, and venues of all types to create one-of-a-kind moments for every couple for whom she has been fortunate enough to be part of their special day.

Her expressive, honed voice, and her years of being in front of crowds as small as 20 and as large as 10,000, have made her a sought after Master of Ceremonies as well. Her easygoing demeanor masks the intense focus she brings to all elements of her events, from pre-planning and sound design to music selection and ideas to get and keep guests interactive and involved.

Her ability to add elements such as a video display, game shows, karaoke and more, make for an even more personalized and interactive experience!

Q: Vanessa, can you tell us about your company and the type of clients you serve?

I am Vanessa Hundley, aka DJ Audioprism, Owner and Head Everything of Audioprism Entertainment in Atlanta, GA. DJ Audioprism was born over a 14 year journey that began in the club scene and has grown into an event specialist and entertainer service. I serve weddings and events of all types and sizes, from backyards to ballrooms.

My clients come to me because they are particular, and they are looking for someone who has skill and knowledge to incorporate their personal music tastes throughout the day.

They also want someone who has extensive event experience and knows how to keep an event flowing, even when things aren't going exactly to plan. They want someone who is engaging and entertaining, yet timely and professional.

Q: How do you go about building your playlist for a wedding?

When it comes to weddings, there is definitely an element of playlist building. But I only have strict playlists for the parts of a wedding that have a definite sequence. The important elements that need to be sequenced include the ceremony music, the music for the Grand Introduction and the special dances, or other specially designated moments that can be enhanced with music.

For the rest of the evening, I build lists filled with the couples' specific requests but they aren't just played in any random order, they are programmed taking the mood and energy in consideration.

That is the part where I use my DJ skills of reading a room and being aware of the current activities to judge when is the best time to play those songs while also mixing in requests from guests.

Q: Do you use a Do Not?

Absolutely! It is your day, your musical way. And if you are just not a fan of that latest hit or even a song from long ago, I want you to feel free to put it on the list. Then, I will politely explain to your friend or family member that while I can't play that, I would be more than happy to see if I could fulfill another request. I can handle that discreetly so that everyone feels good.

Q: What do you feel are the biggest myths or misconceptions about the part a DJ Entertainer plays in the success of a wedding?

There are a few times when I have been approached by someone saying, "We are debating between using a DJ or just using a playlist from (insert any music service/personal library here)".

To some, a DJ appears to be no more than someone who is there to play music. While we are there to play the music, we are also there to use music as a way to create a mood, draw attention to a special moment, get people excited and involved, and so much more.

A great DJ doesn't play just any music at any time, they also must consider their client preferences. You should also expect a great DJ to use their knowledge of music to enhance that selection, and time the music so it is presented at the best moment.

Then there is the element of direction, of informing and guiding guests through the formalities and activities. Simply put, to guide them as to what is going to happen and where their attention should be. Or to announce to the guests what the clients would like them to be doing at a certain time, such as signing a guest book, using the photo booth or gathering for a toast or group picture.

Q: What are some of the most common fears people have about having a successful wedding day working with someone in your profession?

First and foremost, people are worried the DJ won't show up.

It can happen if you're not careful with the DJ you choose. I have received last minute calls from planners and venues in the past reaching out for help in just such cases.

Contracts and referrals are a great step in avoiding this, as DJs willing to provide these take their business more seriously than those who operate on just a reassurance.

Another common fear is of the "showboat" style of DJ taking over the reception and making themselves the center of attention. No one, especially not a newlywed couple, wants to have their day overshadowed by anyone, least of all their entertainment.

What are some of the little known common mistakes that are made when trying to plan a successful wedding day that you would like to make people aware (as it relates to your field)?

A big oversight would be not getting their requests submitted in a timely manner. Doing so allows the DJ time to organize requests and add special songs to their library. DJ's are often working multiple events in a weekend, so last minute song lists and schedules can be challenging to work on in such scenarios. Plus, it allows time for you to discuss your choices with your DJ and be sure they have the correct songs, and the right version you want to hear.

Another blunder is not leaving enough time for special dances/formalities. For example, for introductions, you have to factor in the time needed for getting people in position if necessary, and the actual length of the music choices.

One of the most dangerous oversights is not setting up a clear center of communication for the various vendors. A wedding planner normally does this, but not everyone uses one. It is best to be sure that there is one timeline that every vendor is sent, so that the on the day of things are coordinated smoothly.

How have you been able to help your couples overcome these obstacles?

Over my years of being a DJ I have developed my own music planning form that covers all the essentials of the ceremony and the reception. I also share a free annual resource of popular songs for every part of a wedding compiled by DJ's from across the nation to help them get a feel for the types of songs they may want to use.

Once we have an agreement, I send them both resources and suggest a date night centered around music. During that time, I encourage them to go through and really talk to each other as they explore different music for the day.

I follow up every couple weeks leading up to the date to see how their progress is, if they have any questions or need some suggestions.

After years of weddings and events, I have a very good idea of how long it usually takes for special dances and moments, so as we are discussing those elements I am sure to share that insight for time planning.

I always carry at least 2 printed copies of the schedule with me the day of as well, and compare it to the other vendors' information if I haven't been able to speak to them before then.

Q: What inspired you to become a wedding professional?

Weddings were not initially a huge part of my business focus in the beginning. I was gathering the skills every day though, without realizing it, as I went through different venues and experiences. My first weddings were for friends or people who saw me at a venue, but from the very first one I always thought about how I would want my DJ to treat me, what I would want them to ask and what I thought they might need to know.

Like other life celebrations, a wedding is an important milestone for many and I genuinely enjoy being part of the process and helping them feel at ease with my part of their day!

Q: Can you share a lesson you learned early on, that still impacts how you perform your service today?

I have really worked to streamline my booking process by simply including all the commonly used elements as part of any wedding package.

When I was first getting into weddings and researching how other companies handled their bookings I was instantly overwhelmed by many the offerings and upcharges that I saw. There was a charge for the DJ, a charge for the sound system, a charge for lavalier or wireless microphones, setup fees and teardown fees... that appeared to be the norm.

But after a short while of trying to follow the model and seeing how it could confuse clients as well, I knew I wanted to do something different. I then sat down and thought about everything that I was likely to use during an event and the common scenarios I had seen and designed simple packages with a variety of included common options.

It definitely helped me and my clients have a better understanding of what I was offering and what they were getting. There are still a few add-on options, for people wanting or needing more, but all the basics are covered in the packages.

Q: What's one thing that we may not have covered that you could share with someone who is wanting a successful wedding reception?

I would advise them to meet their prospective DJ in person in advance, if possible. This is not always the case when you are planning a destination wedding, or if your venue or planner offers an all-inclusive package where they handle all of the details for you. However, in those cases, even a phone conversation can avoid a lot of unhappy developments later.

You want to be sure they match their profile picture; that their personality fits the feel you want; then get to know that DJ's background. There are DJ companies who hire talent with no experience, train them for a few weeks and then send them out with a sound system and a playlist. Often with such companies you may not even know who the performer is until the day of. While they may have a "formula", who ever said "I want a wedding like everyone else's"?

Q: How can someone find out more and connect with you?

The hub is, of course, my own website:

www.audioprisment.com. There, you can find contact information, referrals, background information, a schedule of public events I perform at, social media links for your preferred platform and more. Mention this book when booking your wedding and you'll get a complimentary uplighting package or dance light rack with your package (up to $100.00 value)!

SHANNON BUSHEY

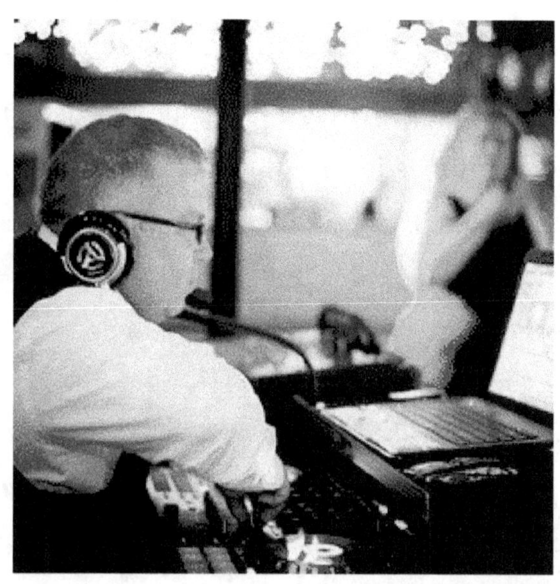

A Conversation with Shannon Bushey
Founder of Digital DJ

Q: What inspired you to become a wedding professional?

I was inspired by watching other wedding professionals, how they worked together as a team and how it all made me feel inside. Weddings for me are like heaven, it's what I was meant to be doing. Every wedding is unique for me, and not just another wedding. Making a couples dream wedding come true, no matter what it takes is what I do.

Q: What are some of the common mistakes that are made when trying to plan a successful wedding day that you would like to make people aware of?

Hiring a friend or a friend of a friend is never a good idea. Just because this person likes music and has some equipment doesn't make him a DJ, or even more so a wedding entertainer. It rarely works out well and that's if they even show up.

Hiring someone with no or very little wedding experience. It's your special day and not the time for do-over's.

Couples wanting to pick each and every song for their reception is a mistake. Although we will allow it, we don't recommend it. Digital DJ always gives our guest of honors the final say. I recommend that they choose their must plays, favorites and ask their family and friends for a few. You should always leave room for requests and the DJ to do what he does best.

Q: How have you been able to help your couples overcome these obstacles?

By telling those real stories of how many couples call us each year frantically because their DJ just cancelled or did not show up on their big day. We tell them this so they don't make the same mistake. We're happy to say we were able to save some of these weddings and are saddened for the ones we could not. We help our couples overcome this by showing them our passion for weddings, our 100% proven track record, our experience and our hundreds of amazing heartfelt reviews. Give your guest a chance to celebrate...with you...and have fun! Digital DJ is passionate about your fun!

Q: Can you share a lesson you learned early on, that still impacts how you perform your service today?

Weddings early on for me seemed very cookie cutter. Everybody wanted the same things and they all seemed alike. So the lesson I learned early on is to be different, meaning being myself and raising the bar even if it meant doing things no one else was doing. Weddings are my passion and today I go the extra mile and out of the box.

I love connecting with our couples and getting to know them personally. It makes a difference and it allows me to make their wedding that much more unique. You will know I've done my job when you see those tears of joy rolling down faces and hear people saying to me, I've never seen that done at a wedding before. These are the memories that will last a lifetime.

Q: What's one thing that we may not have covered that you could share with someone who wants a successful day?

As crazy as this may sound, "It's not all about you!"

Yes it is your special day, but do you want to make it a fun filled and most memorable event of the year? If so, there are many things to consider. Think about your guests and the things they might like to do to include songs they might want to hear while at your wedding. These are the types of things that will show them you care and will make the big difference.

This is the kind of stuff that will get them excited to hit the dance floor and do those silly things that will make the many memorable moments throughout the night! You will be the Heroes of the night and they will thank you over and over for orchestrating this Remarkable Reception!

Q: How can someone find out more and connect with you?

If you would like to see our many reviews you can find them on www.weddingwire.com

You may also connect with us at www.sbdigitalDJ.com. Just for mentioning that you own this book or found us through it we will offer you 1 free upgrade! Contact us now for more details! 802-318-8402.

ADAM SKUBA

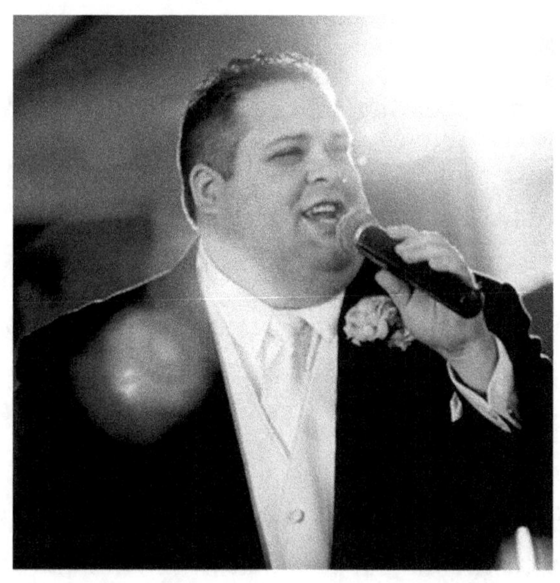

A Conversation with Adam Skuba
of Skuba Entertainment

Adam, tell us about Skuba Entertainment and the types of clients that you serve?

I really enjoy working with clients who have a pretty clear vision of what it is they want for their wedding reception and wedding day. People who have gone to other wedding receptions and have experienced bad wedding entertainment or people that like to watch a lot of the popular wedding TV shows out there that really have a good idea of how they envision their wedding reception to turn out.

I do enjoy working with clients who may not yet have that vision but the clients that have that vision, that have that idea, that have that clear agenda of what they want to accomplish, those are the ones that I have the most success with in creating an exceptional wedding experience for them.

What do you feel is the biggest myth or misconception about DJ entertainers as they play in the success of a wedding?

One thing that I hear a lot from people as they approach the process of hiring a wedding entertainment professional is they think it's just about the music. I hear a lot of questions about, you know this music and that music, and they kind-of just think it's all about the music. One of the things that I have to caution people against is the person that is your wedding MC, your wedding DJ, unfortunately a lot of the responsibility of running that entire reception falls on their shoulders.

Banquet coordinators, venue managers, food and beverage directors, I find that they have one thing in mind and that is get the dinner out and make sure it comes out hot and make sure the guests are happy with the food. They make sure the restrooms are taken care of, that the facility has the air conditioning going or the heat going, but they don't worry about what will make this wedding fun, or what will make this reception fun.

One of the biggest misconceptions is that a DJ Entertainer is just about the music. There's so much more that goes into being the wedding entertainment person, the specialist, the wedding entertainment go-to-guy – like making sure that everything follows a time line, making sure that everything's laid out so we can maximize the amount of fun time that we have at your reception.

One of the things I see happen commonly is everyone comes into a wedding reception with their own goal in mind. One of the things that I try to do before hand is to sit down with everyone, the banquet manager, the photographer if there's a videographer, anybody else that's involved and try to come up with a game plan of how to approach the reception and make up an agenda that will work for everyone.

What happens a lot of times is the photographer will want to grab a sunset picture and maybe that's about the same time that the dinner comes to an end, so you don't want 120 - 150 people sitting around with nothing to do while they take your clients out for a photo. You have to plan for that. I don't think a lot of people think about too much of that going into the reception as much as they concern themselves with what kind of music is he going to play.

What do you find is the most common fear that one of your clients will have about the DJ entertainer?

One of the common fears that I hear that people come to the table with is "what if nobody dances? I just want my wedding to be fun and I want everyone to dance and have a good time."

Again, going back to what I said about creating the timeline -- it's really laid out in order to make sure that everyone's kept involved. Whether they're listening to music or a formality, whether they're eating dinner, whether they're dancing, whether they're watching you do your first dance as a bride and groom, they really need to be involved. I think too many times without the guests involvement, those kinds of receptions tend to, I don't want to call them failures, but they were not primed from the get go to really be something exciting and to really have a successful outcome.

By far the biggest fear is what if we don't have anybody dancing and the best solution for that is to have a great game plan coming in to it.

Can you name one or two common mistakes or pitfalls that you've seen couples make when they're trying to play a successful wedding reception that you'd like to make people aware of?

One of the things I think they misappropriate is the budget. Sometimes I think clients get excited about how their wedding reception is going to actually look. I see a lot of emphasis today in the bridal magazines and especially with the web sites is a lot of emphasis on how the reception looks.

They get caught up in things like picking $200 table clothes or $100 napkins or something like that. By the time they get to the entertainment portion, their budget is completely exhausted.

One of the things that I would urge anyone that is planning a wedding, sit down and figure out what really are the most important things. Are you going just for the way your wedding looks in pictures, or do you really want to create an exciting, exceptional experience for all of your guests to have?

Yes, the linens will look great in the photographs, but nobody walks away from a wedding reception saying, "Boy those table clothes really made me have a good time tonight." That's the one thing that I would urge people to look at overall with the budget.

Then the second thing, getting into the hiring of an entertainment professional -- someone who will work with them and run their reception -- is make sure that you check these people out.

Check this person out, do your research, check for online reviews, ask for video footage of past receptions. The best indicator of future performance is past performance, so anything that they can offer as far as a resume in terms of satisfied client testimonials is absolutely huge.

Those I think are the two biggest things that I would tell couples to look at when they're planning their reception.

Can you give us an example of a way that you've been able to help your couples overcome challenges and have a great reception?

Oh sure, sitting down, everything that I do, and I explain to couples, I'm not one to be so strict with putting together a timeline for the wedding that if I look at my watch and it's 6:01 and we had something scheduled at 6:00 you know the whole thing falls apart. I had a couple that came to me, they were very concerned about making sure their guests danced, making sure everyone had a good time, the reason was the majority of their guests were older. It was on a Sunday afternoon wedding reception and they were concerned that their guests were going to eat lunch/dinner, it was more of an afternoon thing, and pick up and leave.

What I said to them was, perhaps we get a little dancing in before the lunch actually started. They had cocktail hour, they had plenty of appetizers, hors d'oeuvres and drinks, the bar was open. I said you know, those people will not be starving that they have to eat dinner right away, so what about changing the structure of how the afternoon went a little bit to include dancing before dinner. That way if folks did so feel inclined to leave, they would actually have a little bit of fun before they walked out the door.

They loved the idea and it ended up working out really well. I was able to just by addressing their needs of we want to make sure our guests have fun, looking at who their guests were coming to the wedding reception, an older audience, and then renegotiating the time line for the day, make sure that their reception turned out to be something fun.

Now, granted it doesn't fit the mold of what every DJ out there confronts as a great reception, that would be everybody eat and dances to the end the night and screams one more song and whatnot, but success really is making sure that the client is completely satisfied, making sure that the bride and groom are totally happy with the way, and we accomplished that just by changing the order of events a little bit.

Adam, what personally inspired you to become a DJ entertainer and a wedding professional?

Its kind-of a funny story, prior to me, this is pretty much all I've done my entire life. I started in high school, I worked through, I DJ'd parties for other kids I went to school with, a lot of 16th birthday parties and high school graduation parties. I ran into a girl who went to my school, her mom owned a catering facility and she'd asked me if I've ever done a wedding. I said, no, I actually never did a wedding. She said oh it's just like a party, but you read the names. I quickly found out there after that there was a lot more to a wedding reception than just acting as if it was a party.

What really motivated me and inspired me to keep doing this as my livelihood was after I got out of college, I worked at a radio station for a while and I got up to do the morning shift as most interns/first timers in the radio business do, 4:00 in the morning I would go in to do shift from 5:00 in the morning until noon and then go do a wedding reception. I said you know, my clients, my couples deserve better than this than for me to come in like tired and whatnot.

I made a decision and I left radio and I got into the wedding entertainment business full time and I haven't looked back since. I enjoy working with couples of all different backgrounds whether it be ethnicity or their livelihood they pursue, I just like meeting new people all the time. It gives me an opportunity to delve into other people's lives and see what's going on in the world and it's great. It's very self-fulfilling, being able to help someone else look back on what will be the biggest party, the biggest day of their life and know that you were a part of the that and you help make that a success.

Adam can you share a lesson that you've learned early on that still impacts how you perform today?

Gather as much information as possible and don't feel funny, don't feel weird, don't feel that you're being intrusive. Gather at least as far as being an MC of the event, ask the questions that sometimes are a little bit awkward to ask because that will really provide the answers to the bigger picture.

What I mean by all this is, ask what the relationship of what the parents are, or the grandparents. Find out as much details as possible about the family dynamics. You have two families coming together sometimes for the very first time and knowing these family dynamics and planning accordingly can save a lot of hassle and can create actually something absolutely wonderful.

I've learned very early on that ask as many questions as possible, gather up as much information as possible and that will actually help to create a great outcome.

Is there anything that we may not have covered that you'd like to share with a bride or a couple who wants a remarkable reception?

One of the things I think couples in addition to planning that budget, in addition to doing research on the person that you're considering hiring, this is a very personal thing planning a wedding reception. You need to be comfortable as a bride and groom. Your DJ will ultimately be the person who will be representing you in front of your friends and family members on your wedding day.

You need to be comfortable with the person. If you don't feel comfortable with that person, if something's not clicking, if personalities don't mesh, then you might need to look elsewhere. They will be the person on the microphone. They will be the person standing there in front of your family all day and pretty much conducting the entire event for you.

That would be the big thing. You need to, just as you're spending the entire day with your photographer, if the person creeps you out, you don't want to be around them, it probably won't be a good fit around your wedding day. The person that is your DJ, the person that's your MC, the person that's your wedding entertainment professional, you should be comfortable with them. You should know them not only as a professional and what they bring to the table, but I think you need to connect on a personal level as well. That way they set your mind at ease.

You have a lot of things going on, there's a lot of stress on your wedding day, you want to make sure that's not one of them and connecting on that personal level really, really helps ease the fears, the anxieties, any other you know, big problems that you might have. That really just makes it smooth away like butter.

When I get to talk with my clients, I like to find out if they have pets, where they work, what they do for fun, what kind of movies they watch, where they go out to dinner. These are all things that help me connect on a personal level with them. While it may seem insignificant to the actual job that I'm doing, it really helps me to get to know them, and by me sharing information about myself, it helps them get to know me better, which just ultimately ends up being a fantastic relationship.

If folks would like to reach you and learn more, how would they connect with you?

They can shoot me an email over at adam@skubaentertainment.com. I also have a website at http://www.skubaentertainment.com and can be found on Facebook at https://facebook.com/skubaentertainment.

DANNY FARRELL

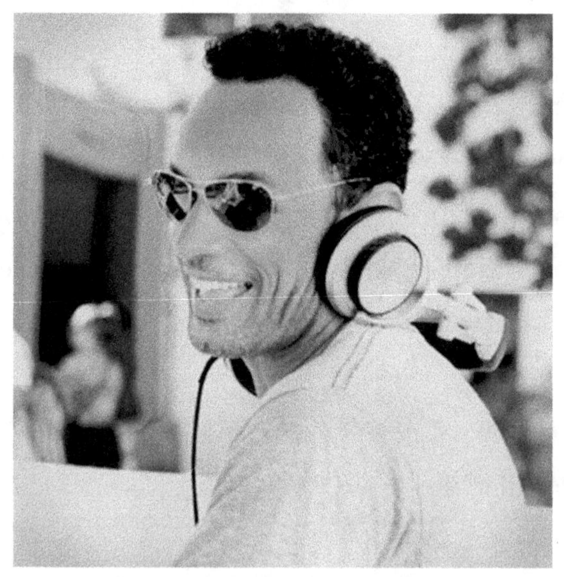

A Conversation with Danny Farrell
Founder of NYC DJ's

Tell us about NYC DJ's and the type of clients that you serve?

I started in New York over 20 years ago, and 14 years ago, I came out to LA, and that's where the company started. In LA, but I named it "NYC DJ's" because the East Coast has a specific style, I think, and that I bring to the West Coast, and I got to use the best of both coasts from what I learned to make the ideal wedding.

Who are the type of clients that seek you out? People that want something different? Tell me about them?

Usually, we attract clients that are fun, quirky, and unique. They are the kind of people that don't want a typical cookie-cutter wedding where everything feels very planned, and there's the same music, and a lot of sitting around and formalities.

We get people that are a little bit creative. They don't want the same wedding that all their friends had or their parents had, for that matter.

Yeah, they're kind of more hip and unique.

What do you feel are the biggest myths or misconceptions about the role a DJ plays in the success of a wedding?

Some of the biggest misconceptions I've come across (and there are many more), are that DJ's just have to press play, they just have an iTunes playlist, they're all the same and they're all corny.

They're not all the same.

I think people can easily lump all DJs into one category, and it may be like I said ... They don't do anything. They just hit "play," and the other side of it is that they're just like a game-show host and just kind of say these cheesy things, and they're not like real people.

What are some of the most common fears people have about having a successful wedding day working with a DJ?

Where so you want me to start Mark? ... I've experienced and helped many clients overcome all sorts of fears. Some of the most common being ... nobody will dance, people will leave early, the DJ will make them look bad, the DJ may embarrass them, show up late, be unprofessional, won't take requests from their guests, the list goes on.

How can clients know that those things won't happen for them? How can they gain confidence?

Because I listen to clients ... I think, anyone who's good at what they do, and when they are exceptional at what they do, they're always open to tweak things and customize things. I don't go in and say, "This is the way it's done. A, B, and C." I'll give my suggestions as to what works, however, I also want to know what's important to my client, and figure how we can make their vision happen.

What are some little-known pitfalls that DJs can fall into while playing a wedding?

Probably by following the wedding playbook of playing the same songs. You know what I mean, the top 100 wedding songs that everyone hears. It's kind of like the blind leading the blind. People are taught a certain style, and DJs just follow that without putting their unique personality into it. Also, knowing the room that you're in is very important, the size of the room and type of guests in that room.

I'll speak differently in a 400-person hall than I will in a 60-person backyard, and it sounds weird if you don't know the room that you're in. Some are more intimate. Some are more of a production, so I think the DJ needs to know who his audience is, who their guests are.

Can you give us an example of how you've been able to help your couples have an unforgettable, smooth, and fun reception?

Number 1, I like to start out with the timeline, the way the whole day is going to flow. I like to mix it up with some formalities and some fun, so that their guests are engaged. For example, a lot of times, they'll bring me a timeline from a venue or from a party planner, and the venue or the party-planner has a specific agenda in mind, and they want to check off their list.

A lot of times that means getting all the formalities out of the way in the beginning, all the toasts, all the food, so they're like, "Okay, my job's done. DJ take over," but as a DJ, I'm there the whole night, and I want what's best for the party. I don't want people to fall asleep. I don't want them to stuff their faces with food and then be like, "Okay, let's dance."

I want to mix that up. I want them to be able to have some fun. I encourage a little bit of dancing before dinner to wake people up, create some energy so that, already, people are like, "Oh, this is kind of different. We don't have to sit through a bunch of speeches and food and toasts before we get to have fun."

Music selection's important. I want people to hear music that they love but that they don't expect to hear at every wedding.

Can you share a lesson that you've learned early on that still impacts early on that still impacts how you perform today?

A lesson I've learned is that it's not about me. I'm there to bring out the best in the crowd, so I do whatever that means, whatever that takes. Sometimes, it's just playing the right song at the right moment. Sometimes, it's just creating a fun environment and letting them do their thing.

Sometimes, I have to do a lot more. I have to get out there. I'm jumping around. I'm showing them a dance. I'm doing something, and I'm using my comedy skills, whatever it takes to break them out of their shell. I have tricks up my sleeve, but I only use what's needed and what's best for that crowd. I'm not there to put on a show. I'm there for them to say, "This was great."

What inspired you to become a wedding professional?

I like the way music brings everyone together. No matter where they're from, no matter what their age is, it can make everyone happy, and it all of a sudden puts everyone on the same page. When people are dancing, it's hard to have a frown on your face. You naturally kind of smile and be a little silly, so I like what it does to people, no matter what's going on in their lives.

We're there because someone fell in love, and we're celebrating that, so it's really just a great energy. A lot of positive vibes, so we're celebrating something positive, and there's just a lot of happiness, and it affects people, it's a lot of smiling faces, and I like that. It's better than working in the DMV.

What's one thing that we may not have covered that you could share with someone who wants to have a successful wedding day and wants to have the right entertainer?

I think that people should really think about how they can bring their own personality into their wedding and not just listen to wedding forums and other people's advice. It's good to listen to advice, but anything's possible, so if they have an idea in their head or a vision that they would like, I would say work with a DJ who is willing to try and figure out a way to make that happen.

True professionals will listen to them and work with them on how to create that as opposed to, "No, no, no, you can't do that. This is the way to do it."

If people do not have a specific idea, then great. Then they can have professional suggest things. If they have many great ideas, I think they should run them by the DJ so they can help figure out a way to make it happen.

What is your philosophy on how you like to run your business?

My philosophy is I like to run my business thinking about what I would want if I were the client, and I am very picky in my life with things that I purchase, and people that I hire.

Simply by saying, "What would I want," it makes me constantly raise the stakes and challenge myself and step things up because I don't want something that's typical. I want something that's extraordinary, so if I always ask myself "What would I want. How would I want this service? How would I want this to go?" Then, it keeps me on top of my game.

What's the best way for a bride or a groom to connect with you, learn more and contact you?

I always like to have a conversation rather than just an email, so whether it's a phone call, a Skype or an in-person meeting, I like to get to know my prospective clients and hear what's important to them. Sometimes, if it's just an email, it can be very impersonal, like, "How much for this?"

I want to hear more about their likes and dislikes, so yeah, I would say phone call, Skype, meeting, whatever's best for their schedule. They can reach me at 323-204-3138. They can get a lot of information on my website. There's videos. There's music mixes. Testimonials.

The website is www.nyc-DJs.com

FREDERICK HART

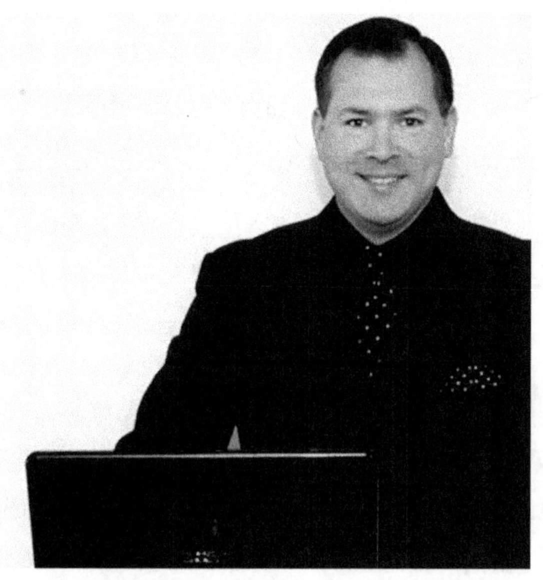

A Conversation with Frederick Hart
of Frederick Hart Entertainment, LLC

Frederick tell us about your business and the types of clients you serve.

My company, Frederick Hart Entertainment LLC, offers a highly specialized and customer specific expertise that is dedicated to providing every bride with a precise interpretation of HER vision rather than a contrived "cookie cutter" approach where a wedding reception is little more than a carbon copy of the one before it.

My brides have unique tastes, particular opinions, and very high expectations for the one special day that she has been imagining since her first crush at age 12. Through my training, experience, skill, and inventiveness, her imagination happens in real life. The responsibility of creating the most important day in her life (eclipsed, perhaps, only by giving birth), rests squarely upon my shoulders. It's a role that I appreciate. A duty that I relish.

What do you feel are the biggest myths or misconceptions about the role your service plays in the success of a wedding?

To the uninitiated, the DJ just plays music. It's not unusual for a bride to conclude that if she picks ALL of the songs for her wedding reception, she can rent a sound system, plug in her laptop, and have a euphoric celebration that all of her guests will enjoy. Perhaps she'll hire the most economical DJ to play her songs and check them off the list. It's a recipe that virtually guarantees a disaster.

It's tragic to hear of a wedding that ends early due to the guests leaving because of inexperienced or untalented entertainment. My presence is the insurance policy that ensures my client gets every penny's worth of their wedding reception by keeping the guests engaged, involved, and entertained until the last song of the evening.

What are some of the most common fears people have about having a successful wedding day working with someone in your profession?

No guest ever attends a wedding reception to see the DJ. They go for the bride and / or groom but far too many DJs (in my market of Philadelphia/Southern NJ, at least) don't seem to appreciate that fact and try to become the star of the show. The clients are so jaded from experience that they figure that they should hire a band if they wish to have a tasteful and classy wedding reception.

DJs are notorious for acting buffoonish, showing off, and hogging the spotlight and the last thing that my brides want is a loud and obnoxious attention starved caricature of a personality (with a wrestling announcer's inflection and enthusiasm) creating a circus atmosphere at HER wedding reception.

What are some of the little known pitfalls / common mistakes that are made when trying to plan a successful wedding day that you would like to make people aware?

Many of my clients are extremely organized. Some are TOO organized. Adhering to the schedule as annotated in their extremely detailed itinerary isn't advisable and will at best awkwardly apply to the dynamics of a crowd.

On numerous occasions, the dance floor was packed with EVERY guest dancing at the scheduled time for cake cutting. When the energy level is so peaked, it's a huge mistake to suddenly pull the plug for an activity.

As an adept DJ, I can select songs to control the energy level or simply wait until the crowd needs to cool off and introduce the cake cutting ceremony a few minutes AFTER the dictates of the schedule. The itinerary may read that the cake cutting is at 9:00 but the dance floor sometimes says otherwise.

How have you been able to help your couples overcome these obstacles?

Of my numerous roles and responsibilities at a wedding reception, the job of event planner is 2nd most critical. It is important to create a customized schedule to smoothly usher the guests through the announcements, toasts, meal presentation, specialty dances, activities (cake cutting, garter / bouquet toss) and still have sufficient time for dancing and celebrating.

Catering managers and Maîtres'd are focused mainly on the speed and timing of feeding guests. They have copious amounts of expertise in food service but little to no experience in entertainment and the reality is that a wedding reception is an entertainment event.

The entertainment will determine whether it is a rousing success or a bleak and embarrassing failure.

What inspired you to become a wedding professional?

From 1989 – 2001, DJ'ing weddings was a well-paying and fun weekend side job that acted as a counterbalance to the real estate tax lien investment "career job" that occupied my weekdays but left me emotionally unfulfilled. My moment of epiphany came in August of 2001 when volunteering at the Ronald McDonald Camp for children being treated for or recovering from cancer.

I was lucky to DJ "CAMP JAM", a dance on the last night of the week long camp. A very homesick child who refused to participate in activities all week was fascinated by the equipment and lights and became my assistant for the night. No counselor succeeded in getting him to engage or "come out of his shell" all week but, with the help of music, I did.

It remains the defining moment that inspired me to pursue wedding entertainment full time. I resigned from my "day job" two weeks later and still volunteer / donate my time each year to the fundraising efforts of at least 10 different organizations.

Can you share a lesson you learned early on, that still impacts how you perform your service today?

My mantra from the beginning has been "it's NOT MY wedding". Getting to know my clients gives me critical insight about their tastes, style, preferences, and personalities which allows me to customize every aspect of their event. My only focal point is the bride and how well I follow her instructions and respect HER vision. I won't show up at a wedding and then deliver MY ideal version of the perfect wedding reception. I'm sworn to my boss in the white dress. Surpassing her expectations is paramount at EVERY wedding. 1,800 to date and counting.

What's one thing that we may not have covered that you could share with someone who is wanting a successful day (as it relates to your field)?

A wedding DJ is not just the person playing music. There are many other critically important responsibilities that must be mastered. To be exceptional he / she must also act as the host, announcer, master of ceremonies, event coordinator, AND the person who plays music.

Find and hire an experienced professional and DON'T seek out the best bargain. The difference between a seasoned veteran and an inexperienced dilettante is only a few hundred dollars but the COST of a bad wedding that ends early or is a complete debacle is considerable.

How can someone find out more and connect with you?

I eagerly welcome the opportunity of providing my service to discerning bridal clientele throughout the U.S. and abroad and can be easily found at http://www.fhentertainment.com.

GRANT BRICKNER

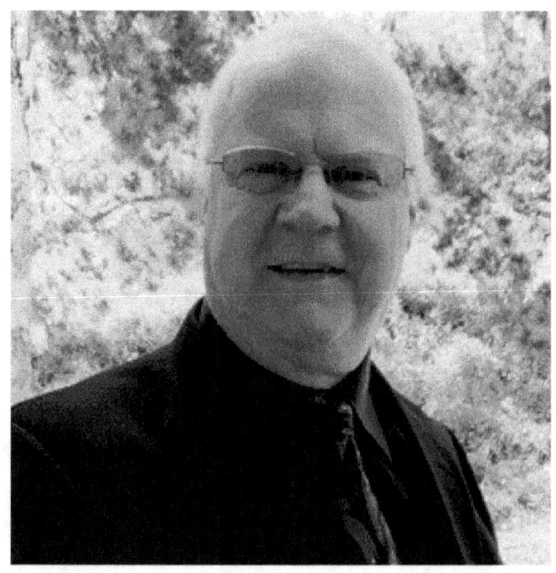

A Conversation with Grant Brickner
of Accent Weddings and Events

Grant Brickner is the owner of Accent Weddings And Events. He grew up being exposed to a wide range of music, from Big Band, to the Classic Standards, Motown, Folk, Classic Country, Rock and even Punk. He discovered DJing early on and soon found out his background in Communications and Stand-up Comedy translated perfectly into being a DJ.

His vast knowledge of music, coupled with his skills and expertise as a Master Entertainer and Emcee, have made his unique talents highly sought after by customers and their guests alike, in a professional career spanning over 30 years and thousands of events.

Grant, there are so many DJs, what questions should I ask of them to find the "pearl among the oysters?"

Grant Brickner: This book will provide a myriad of possible questions you can ask. However it's important to note that comparing DJs is not apples to apples. It's more like apples to oranges. It's up to you, the client to give the DJ your parameters so that you can create a real comparison.

First, give them a date, location and a standard time frame of say, 4 hours. (These are factors that can affect pricing.) Do they charge a package price or by the hour? Ask what services they offer in that package. Are there any other charges like travel, early set up or for a sound system for the ceremony?

Next, find out what their deposit amount is, what their overtime rate per hour is, and when is your final balance due. Do they have professional DJ insurance? Most importantly, ask if they provide a contract or agreement, this protects you AND them. If they don't, keep looking! (Be sure to read and understand it.

Always ask questions if you are unsure of any part.) Lastly, are they an information giver or did they ask you questions? Did they show an interest in you? This is the area where your professional Entertainers/DJs separate themselves from being a commodity (one price fits all DJ) and excel as a specialized service (specific to your needs and wants). This is where YOU will start to form your "let's set up an interview list".

What makes your company different?

Our years of experience (the best teacher) and reliability. We had operated for over 22 years as part of the Nation's largest entertainment franchise and we have a proven positive service record. The problem was, that it was a "cookie cutter" waY of doing things. I found that as we added additional services, we were unable to adapt to specific requests that our clients wanted. This caused me much consternation. I came to the realization that to be a company that people wanted to use, we had to adapt to our clients wishes in a timely manner. I saw this as an opportunity to start a new business model, where we are adaptive and responsive to our customer's needs.

We now utilize only established and experienced professionals as our team members. Our quality of ongoing training sets us apart in maintaining and delivering a positive and consistent customer service experience.

How do I know that you'll make my event a success?

Grant Brickner: We keep it simple, we have two goals. Firstly, to make sure your plans are followed and secondly, to make sure you and all your guests have a great experience.

By using and following the Planning Sheets, asking detailed questions and information sharing with associated vendors, we are able to stay connected with the flow and content of your event. This also allows us the ability to quickly and positively adapt to changes that arise.

How do I know what services I need and that you won't try sell me more?

Grant Brickner: Simple, it's your choice. You are the only one who knows what you need, want and ultimately what you will afford. We offer you information on our entire line of services so that you can make the decision that's right for you. That is precisely why we bundle our products, so that you can enjoy more services, with the benefit a team of professionals to manage it all for you.

Tell us about Accent Weddings and Events and the types of clients you serve?

Grant Brickner: Accent Weddings And Events is a San Diego based, multi-service entertainment company that evolved out of a successful franchise model in 1993.

We offer DJ/Emcees, Photography, Videography, Photo Booth & Event Lighting Services. We serve both private, corporate and military customers, but we primarily specialize in weddings and receptions. From the newly engaged couples, the seasoned catering managers, to event planners and wedding coordinators; our model is to provide a stress-less, one-stop shop for all the entertainment services we provide.

Originally, we were just a DJ service. However, with my years of personal experience in corporate entertainment and weddings, it naturally led me to incorporate more associated services, providing increased entertainment options for my clients. Once we diversified our services, we immediately began to receive even more positive input from our clientele. Our version of the "one-stop entertainment shop" has really filled a need.

What do you feel are the biggest myths or misconceptions about the role your service plays in the success of a wedding?

Misconception Number One: I don't need a budget, how much could it cost anyway?

The first thing you'll discover is that what you thought things cost and what they do cost is way different. Welcome to the world of wedding planning! Once you catch your breath, you'll want to get serious about having a realistic budget and sticking to it.

Having a number you think you want to pay is not a budget. Developing a budget is the single most important thing you can do. It takes work and research. You'll need to make calls and determine what the average going rate is for the items you want, so you can form your budget on realistic numbers that you've encountered.

After researching your costs, first, determine what you can afford and are willing to spend on the day. Second, determine what items you must have in order of importance, such as, (wedding dress, formal attire, officiate, location, food, entertainment etc.) Third, determine what items you would like to have based on costs (party favors, linens, centerpieces, etc.) Fill the 'must haves' first and the 'like to haves' with the balance.

Misconception Number Two: All DJs do the same thing.

False. Sure, anyone can play music, (why should I pay you, when I've got a friend, cousin etc. that will do it for free?) The main reason is simple. They are not trained professionals with real experience. Hall managers, wedding coordinators, and previous brides will all readily volunteer that “the DJ will make or break the event”. Surveys consistently show that six months after a wedding, your reception entertainment is still the NUMBER ONE thing your guests will remember about your wedding.

Experience wins. You can't fake it. Every DJ has had their share of mistakes and hopefully learned some valuable lessons along the way, but it's the inexperienced DJ that continues to make more mistakes, doesn't learn from them and ultimately ruins events and creates the "horror stories" you hear about.

A good DJ knows his music and how to use it to change the mood and the energy. They know how to command an audience, they sound smooth and clear on the microphone and use proper English. They know how to multi-task, juggling input from the host, guests and vendors and still keep the event on time and on course.

An inexperienced DJ, will have a poor presence and be ineffective on the microphone, will struggle with continuity, interrupt the flow of the event with poor segues and miss important details that affect the overall perception of your quests. DJ'ing may seem like an easy task, however it is not as easy as many people would believe. Like with any occupation, the professionals make it look that way.

Unless you're buying a home, a yacht or a luxury automobile, you'll most likely never spend this much on a single event in your life as you will for your wedding. Nor will it have this kind of emotional impact on you. The old adage still holds true; you get what you pay for. The secret is to buy what you want, only after you determine what it is that you need.

The DJ makes the party, the Photographer captures the moments and the Videographer tells the rest of the story. If you have a novice, inexperienced photographer or videographer, it may or may not affect the final product they produce. However, if the entertainer isn't experienced, you will see, hear and experience each and every mistake they make in real time. It will completely affect the energy and the flow of your event.

Misconception Number Three: Price doesn't determine outcome.

On the low side, it absolutely does. On the high side, it certainly can. Let me use this analogy: Your wedding day is like renting a car for a long trip. You are going to put all your effort, hard earned money, everything you've planned, worked for, hoped for and expect, into this car. Do you want Economy or Luxury?

Now they both get you to your destination. But in what condition will you find yourself in when you get there? With the Economy model you have no regrets about what you paid, you may have to sacrifice reliability and make do without certain things. You are left with a ride that's bumpy and uncomfortable that you can't wait to be over.

With the Luxury ride you paid more, but during this ride you get to experience reliability and the smooth, relaxing, enjoyable extras that leave you grateful and pleased you opted for more. Having worked alongside many non-professionals over the years, I speak from experience when I tell you that your guests will most certainly notice the difference.

In a major survey that queried brides before and after their wedding, found that before the wedding, brides placed their reception entertainment as the 9th most important item. But after the wedding, over 90% of those same brides said that their entertainment choice should have been their NUMBER ONE priority, and of those brides, over 70% said they should have spent more on their entertainment.

What are some of the most common fears people have about having a successful wedding day working with someone in your profession?

The DJ will ruin our day or worse yet embarrass us. No one wants a DJ that's cheesy or one that only plays what he wants to hear. Certainly no one wants to be singled out over the microphone either. These are things that inexperienced Entertainers do. We operate with the mindset that it is never about us, it's always about you.

Your comfort level and enjoyment comes first. All of our announcing is done with one purpose only: To focus the attention of the audience to the next event. Fear should NEVER be part of the equation. A little apprehensiveness is normal. But that's our job to fix, by building a relationship of trust with our customers.

All DJ's pressure sell you. It's unfortunate that there are some DJ's that certainly do that. That's exactly why many are just DJ's, because they are not good salesmen. You can't force a fit, that doesn't work for anyone and it reeks of desperation.

First, we always seek to educate our brides and grooms. Then we let you the customer, make an informed decision about what feels right to you. At the very least, you can move forward better equipped to make informed and educated choices. We understand that we aren't everyone's entertainment service and not everyone is our customer. We have even referred customers to other services that we thought would be a better fit for them!

What are some of the little known pitfalls / common mistakes that are made when trying to plan a successful wedding day that you would like to make people aware of?

Grant Brickner: I'll just have my "friend/family member" make some calls for me. This is probably the single biggest mistake you can make. Don't ask someone else to make your calls for information for you. While well intentioned, this person may omit or misunderstand important key details that may affect your final decision.

Why would you risk all your effort, time, plans and the major financial investment you've made, only to have important details overlooked? You're relying on your entertainer to represent you, to your friends and family, by all means get to know them!

Ignoring or overlooking this valuable fact gathering detail is a learning experience that can have far-reaching effects on the success of your event. This is one of the most important days of your life; YOUR wedding day! No one knows what you want more than you. Invest in yourself. Do your own research.

Don't place too much importance/money/effort into things that will not have much effect on the outcome of the wedding. Things like party favors, table linens, seating charts, menu options, etc. can seriously affect your bottom line and lead to added stress.

If you place too much importance on the small things, stress can steal your day. Understand that it's not going to be perfect. It has a life of its own. Plan what you can and have a professional team you trust. Then sit back, let go, relax and enjoy what you've created!

Be organized. Your vendors are busy and they have to be organized. When you're not, it makes their job more difficult and that can lead to problems. Get yourself a note book and take lots of notes so you know what is included and provided. This will help you keep the important details right where you need them in finalizing your plans

Avoid having too much time between ceremony and reception. This is a celebration killer! Keep it short, 90 minutes or less. Example, taking pre-ceremony pictures can help. At the reception, keep your wedding party on a short leash until the scheduled dances are done. Chasing them down can waste valuable time and disrupt the event. Another important item: If you have a drinking crowd, keep your bar where your guests are. Nothing will drain the energy of an event like splitting the gathering areas.

How have you been able to help your couples overcome these obstacles?

Grant Brickner: We interview our clients with the 'imagine your day' scenarios, where we ask open ended questions to reach the most important details. For example; What do you see? What are your fears? Where are your joys? We ask the Bride and/or Groom about what family moments they envision and would like to see. These answers provide us with better insight into how we can incorporate songs, announcements or group activities that will bring even greater meaning to the event.

We utilize detailed planning sheets to help organize and set a working timeline and identify key participants. These planning sheets also provide us with coordination information that we use to work with the other vendors to ensure cooperation and success for ceremonies, receptions and other events.

Events can often do and go off their timeline. We offer advice and creative options on how to consolidate different events at ceremonies and receptions to assist saving or making up time, allowing you more time to visit and socialize.

What inspired you to become a wedding professional?

Grant Brickner: While in the U.S.A.F. overseas, I tried my hand at comedy at the base level talent contest. I ended up winning at the Base, Then All England and finally, All Europe level). From then on I was hooked! I loved being in front of an audience and was always looking for that opportunity.

A few years later, after planning my own wedding with some less than desirable results, I was left wondering how it could have been better. I was looking at wedding advertisements for ideas and came across an ad for a Disc Jockey trainee. I was hired at the interview, suited up and began my journey. That quickly evolved into wanting to be part of something larger. To be a part of someone else's success and to be remembered as someone who helped make a great lifetime memories. That's when I realized I had found my true path.

Can you share a lesson you learned early on, that still impacts how you perform your service today?

Grant Brickner: When I got my first job at 14, my Grandfather sat me down, gave me some advice that his Father had given to him. It had a great impact on me and has been a path I have tried to show to others. He said, "There is honor in work. Your work speaks for who you are as a person. Doing less than your best is a direct reflection of your character that everyone can see. If you don't like your work, you can change it, but never give less than what you would expect from yourself."

He also told me that, "You are responsible for all you do and people will judge you for that. If you give your word, do what you said you would do. If you don't like the deal you made, you can only blame yourself. Next time make a better deal, but never do less than what you promised."

Remembering to stay humble and grateful, it's never about me, it's always about the client and what will make them the happiest. I still love having the ability to lead an audience to a fun place where they smile, laugh and dance, where they can let go of their worries.

What's one thing that we may not have covered that you could share with someone who is wanting a successful day?

Grant Brickner: I learned this at my own wedding, don't plan too much activity at your wedding! You can still keep your guests involved, even with less structure. I sometimes ask clients, how would you feel if your guests left early during your event? This is something that can and does happen.

Putting in too many items will leave no time for the party everyone is expecting. Your celebration has a life of its own, allow it to be fluid. Remember that you've spent months, weeks and days planning your minutes and seconds. It's going to go by quicker than you could have imagined. Be present in the moment, look at what you've created, enjoy and have fun!

How can someone find out more and connect with you?

Grant Brickner: Sure, they can reach me at 619-464-3344. They can visit my website for more information at www.accentweddingsandevents.com, or they can email me at accentwae@gmail.com

If you took the time to read our portion of this book, we'd like to say thank you and we've got a special discount reward just for you. Simply mention this book when you call.

JOHN D'ANGELO

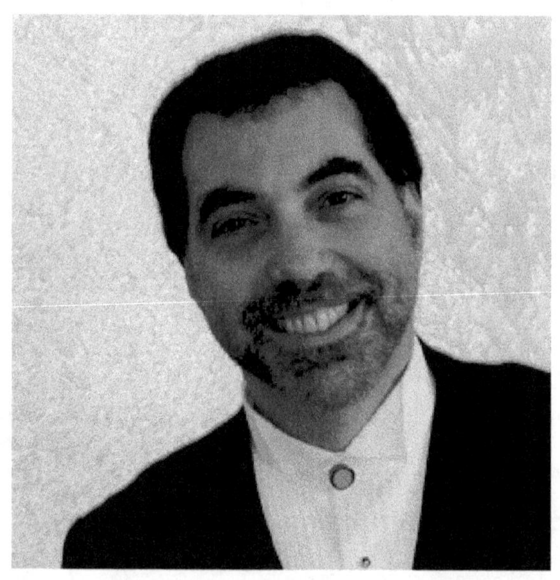

A Conversation with John D'Angelo
of A Perfect Wedding DJ

A Perfect Wedding DJ is a solely-owned and operating Disc Jockey company ran by John D'Angelo. He provides music for all occasions, but focuses mostly on the Wedding Experience.

When you speak with him, you're garnering the trust and confidence of a seasoned professional who's spent over 20 years helping clients plan, prepare and execute their special event.

Having incredible experience and with over 4000 events behind him; there is no substitute as John D'Angelo is most certainly "A Perfect Wedding DJ".

Tell us about your business and what you do.

My business is A Perfect Wedding DJ and I help brides and grooms that invest 20K or more in their wedding celebrations to assure their big day runs smoothly.

I do that through a unique format of production staging, including full-service planning and coordination of their wedding reception and entertainment, from formal announcements to execution of their entire event.

How did you get started in Wedding Entertainment?

Funny story how I got started! It actually started 4 decades ago when I was speaking in the hallways of Middle School and one of the English/Drama teachers said "you should be on radio". Didn't have a clue what she meant, but simply said "yeah, thank you". I was already involved with the various music, acting and theater departments back then and kept on dabbling in that field.

Fast forward 20 years; while working on the docks, made an announcement on the PA system and the same thing happened; this big, burly, intimidating looking inspector walked up asked "was that you making that announcement? My mind flashed "oh, you're in deep trouble John" as I answered yes. Then he said "why are you not on radio?"

At that moment I felt "maybe these people have a point and it's time to start looking". I answered a newspaper ad about being on the radio and I ended up creating my "own" radio station by becoming a mobile disc jockey entertainer.

After that, no matter what job I held in corporate America, the same comments always came up: "you should be on radio, you should be announcing on TV".

How has your background and experience shaped your business?"

I've participated in, directed and produced many musical productions from 'Fiddler on the Roof, The Music Man, Hello Dolly, Camelot, 1776 & South Pacific' just to name a few. Producing, directing and blocking a wedding reception utilize many of the same techniques as a musical production.

Each section of the reception needs to be planned out as though it is an act in a musical production because quite honestly it is. Think about it for a second Mark, the entire concept is remarkably similar; people will be talking, making speeches, dancing, some may even break out into song when the right music is played. How are these two entities not similar?

So really what a couple should look for is someone who can properly structure and pace each section of their event. Without that type of proper planning and interaction with the various vendors, their event could fall short of its real potential to be extraordinary.

What makes you different?

For those brides who have spoken with me at bridal shows or read through enough of my e-mails that I send out, they understand my philosophy, my take, my outlook on what a wedding is all about. I say it all the time; weddings are nothing less than a musical production.

A while back, FOX Network aired the live musical production of 'Grease'. I tell you this not to see if you watched to see who the guy was that played John Travolta's role or the girl who played Olivia Newton-John's part. I tell you this because of the commentary that happened between the show (part of the commercials if you will) of the PRODUCTION of this live musical.

They explained what it actually took to make the musical happen, how all the moving parts came together to create what you saw on the show. It actually gave you an insight as to how your wedding could be handled if you enroll the help of a Wedding Producer (not just a DJ or an Entertainment Company), but a person who can actually help you create, produce, direct, narrate and execute your wedding.

Here's a real example.

I recently signed a person who works on the set of Blue Bloods (yes that cop show with Tom Selleck). She spoke with me once at a bridal show. When I mentioned to her 'HOW' I pull together all the parts of her wedding reception, she immediately wanted to meet with me to discuss her wedding in greater detail. I had NO idea she worked on the set until after her signing with me. She told me afterwards that she contracted me BECAUSE OF THE WAY I HANDLE WEDDING EVENTS! It was exactly the way they work on set and she saw my 4 decades of Production experience and two decades of Mobile Wedding experience as a HUGE plus and the PERFECT way to bring her wedding ideas to life.

So what's the take-away to this event?

I tell a story of how two people meet & fall in love. I do that with music & song & dance. Not just with words. It's an age-old story, boy meets girl, boys kisses girl, boy falls in love with girl & we have a big party. Now, they could just elope, exchange some spoken vow & call it a day, but wouldn't it be nicer & more dramatic, more memorable if they took it to the next level? That's where I come in.

Let me explain it this way.

What I do is help couples see the entire aspect of their event thru the eyes of a camera. I want them to be able to see how their story unfolds as we play it out onto a big screen. Do you want to know why I do it that way? Because if they are being photographed or videotaped by anyone, their entire event can be re-lived through those photos & videos.

I want those memories to be as special as possible. If a couple are spending $5,000-10,000 on photography & video, doesn't it make sense that the entertainment needs to be at the very best level in order for the other two services to have something of quality to capture?

If the entertainment falls short, the other two vendors will be a waste of time & money & the entire event is destroyed. You need to have someone with a producer's eye, a director's eye; someone who can see what the final product could look like. That's what I do, I help them visualize their day completely; I help them see what could be. I make their dreams become reality.

It's not a short process. It takes time. Time to talk, time to listen, time to make decisions along the way. Most people come to understand what I'm saying if I state it this way; I look at their wedding as though it were a movie. Really & truly, it's actually a musical. Some people get it, those that were in theater or drama back in high school or college. They understand, this is a musical of their life, their day.

For some people, if they were more on the athletic side, this is the game, the big show. It takes time, practice & effort to get there. It takes someone who can guide you as well. That's where I come in.

With over 20 years of mobile entertainment & 4 decades of general entertainment background, I use my skills as a director, a producer to create each event uniquely suited for each couple's dream. Like a fine suit, each event is custom, tailor made.

Now, some couples don't want all the fuss of a big show. They are looking for good entertainment. Who better than someone with a creative eye, a great sense of rhythm & timing; someone who can see what others don't, should be chosen to handle even a more relaxed type of event?

Tell me what the biggest challenge or misconception couples have today when it comes to planning their wedding receptions?

Couples underestimate how important the planning process is, how their DJ is not only their Master of Ceremonies, but also is the Entertainment Director, the Wedding Coordinator for the entire reception.

A common misconception is that the DJ is just the music or that it's "just a 4 hour party". The fact of the matter is the Entertainment is coordinating between the Maitre D, the Photographer, the Videographer, the bride and groom, all the guests. The DJ Entertainer is not only the person providing music, but because they're the one with the microphone, they're the Wedding Director and Producer.

They're the one that is actually setting the tone, the speed and the rhythm of the entire event. Do it correctly, and you can see opportunities that can turn an ordinary wedding into something that is extraordinary and magical. As a result, it's not uncommon for me to spend anywhere from 35-55 hours of preparation time for and with a client prior to the event to make certain everything goes even better than the way the couple expected.

What is the number one thing a couple should look for when choosing an Entertainer or DJ for their big day?"

Couples should understand that it isn't "just" entertainment they are looking for. Linked to my previous comments about how your DJ Entertainer is your Entertainment Director, they also are representing YOUR style as a couple, and you want to find an entertainer that puts YOUR theme and YOUR style as a priority over their idea of entertainment.

You'll want to speak or meet with the entertainer and find out if they match you as a couple, and if they actually care to hear your ideas and themes for your reception, or if they're willing to help if you want ideas for your theme. They're playing the soundtrack of YOUR lives, not theirs.

Look for vendors that are committed to advance planning. They should work closely to each client to share a common vision of the event's success. Remember, great wedding receptions don't 'just happen', they involve hours of planning for each hour of performance time.

And look for someone who can properly prepare and create timeline. Look for signs whether they care about anything other than the music, that they care about the people who are attending the event and how they could respond to various songs, lights or effects that can happen at a wedding. Finally, look for someone who is paying attention to your wants, needs and desires and is in tune with you, the client, not just themselves handling the same old, cookie-cutter wedding format.

What are the biggest pieces of advice you can give a couple who are planning their big day?

Find someone who is passionate, someone that loves what they do. Look for someone who holds nothing back, who's not afraid of a crowd that may not be in their pocket. Move towards people who can see things others can't and who can turn that vision into reality. Find someone who will listen first and then ask questions that will lead you to a successful event, someone who is fully committed. Look for someone who can make the impossible possible and see the potential in the event that you might not see yourself.

Plan far enough in advance that decisions aren't made because 'it's the last minute, I have to find someone noooooow'. Please don't be the bride, and there always seems to be quite a few like this, who call 2 or 3 months out from their date looking for entertainment, begging vendors for anyone and they get the 'leftovers'. (Mark, go back to your high school days, those are the people that are the last to get picked for sides on any sports team.) When you as a wedding couple are spending 15, 25, maybe 35 thousand, why would you make that one mistake of going for leftovers?

Make certain that you, as a couple assemble your "team" of vendors in such a way that you can enjoy every minute and be “in-the-moment”, knowing every detail will be handled for you so you can relax and enjoy your celebration and 'be' with your guests, rather than having to "work" your own wedding.

What was the most challenging wedding reception you've ever done?

On multiple occasions, I’ve been called on Emergency from a couple who hired a DJ that either canceled, disappeared on them, or they simply didn’t know the importance of preparation for a couple’s big day. I’ve been called in with less than a day to prepare. Fortunately, I was able to learn the family dynamic, their style, and music and create a timeline that suited the day. It isn’t easy, but can be done.

The takeaway is to book the entertainment as early in your planning as possible for two reasons:

1) Because your entertainer can be your point-person for suggestions on other aspects of your reception planning.

2) Because popular entertainers can be booked up to 18 months in advance, and you want to lock them in with a professional contract, so you won’t end up in an emergency situation like this.

How can brides connect you and learn more about working with you?

For a bride planning their wedding reception, preferably 6 to 15 months ahead, although I can also help a last-minute couple if needed, they can get a complimentary 'Dream Wedding Design Session' with me.

They will find all the details at: http://aperfectweddingDJ.com or they can send an e-mail to john@aperfectweddingDJ.com to schedule time, or call me at 973-257-0405 for even faster results.

Now, for those couples who aren't ready to make a commitment yet, but want to find out more about me or get more information from me; they can send an e-mail to moreinfo@aperfectweddingDJ.com.

By doing that, they will be placed onto my e-mail service and get helpful tips and insights to help them plan their big day.

STEVE BENDER

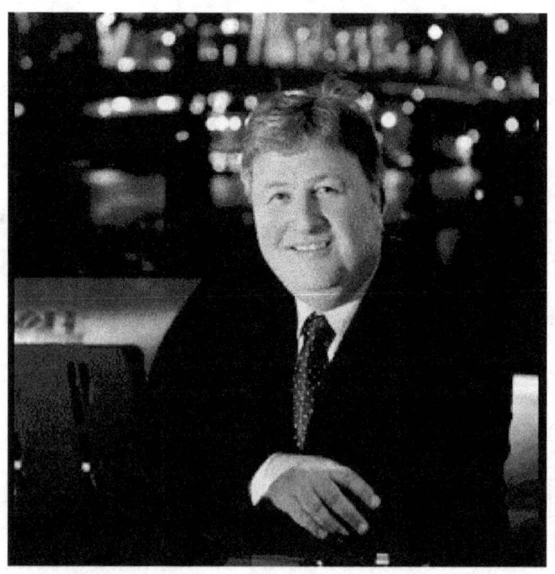

A Conversation with Steve Bender
of Steve Bender Entertainment

Tell us about your business and the type of clients that you serve?

We are a professional entertainment service. DJ service is our primary focus. We've been in business, at this point, basically 40 years. We provide quality entertainment services with DJs. We have photo booths. We just added on something new, a character artist, things of that nature, all focused on the wedding industry. lighting, uplighting, and monograms. We aren't involved in decor and so forth like some companies are but that's our primary focus.

Our clients are brides. They make up about 90% of our business where we focus mainly on weddings, whether it be the wedding reception and/or ceremonies. We also do corporate events, private parties. Our typical client is someone in the 18 to 34-year old age group, which is our primary demographic from which we attract most of our clients from.

We would probably be considered in our marketplace, in terms of price point, we would probably be primarily in that middle to middle-high category depending upon options that they add. We're known for high quality, we're known for experience, and we're known for being able to give great value for the price.

What do you feel are the biggest myths or misconceptions about the role a DJ entertainer plays in the success of a wedding?

The biggest myth in terms of what I think probably most people have a myth or expectation about is that you're just up there, and you're just going to play some songs off of a list that somebody provides, and anybody can basically do it. Typically, everybody has a friend or a friend of a friend who, oh yeah, they DJ. They do this on the side. When it comes to equipment, when it comes to just hitting a button and playing the song, that's true. I mean, anybody can do that, but it's somebody special that knows how to play the right songs at the right time and grow the crowd in terms of what you see on the dance floor.

More importantly, it's very important for a DJ to know what not to do. I think the greatest myth, for me at least, what I've seen over the 40 years I've been doing this, is the belief that ... You know, I got a friend. He's a DJ or she's a DJ. We're just going to hire them because 'all you're really doing is just playing some songs. We don't need anything special.'

My thought is it's your special day so why would you not want it to be the best it could possibly be? You're not going to skimp typically on food. You're not going to skimp usually on the dress and the things of that nature. Entertainment ... I think Martha Stewart said it, "Entertainment, basically, will determine 80% of your event's success." I'm a firm believer in that.

What are some of the most common fears that brides have working with a DJ entertainer like yourself?

The biggest fears I found that brides are usually on the brides' part. Brides are worried. They worry about, "Will my DJs show up on the day? What happens if they get sick? What happens if there's an accident or if the equipment breaks and so forth?"

One of the biggest things that I did back in the old days was, at bridal shows, I would literally have music playing in my booth very softly in the background. It's worth mentioning at this stage, that during my presentation, I typically have four, five, six couples talking in front of me.

I would bring up the fact ... Literally, I would visually, physically do this. I'd be talking and talking about your DJ's there, they're playing your music. Then, all of a sudden, boom! Power amp goes out. I turn off the power amp and the music goes blank. One moment there's music playing and all of a sudden, there's no music.

Often, when something like this happens, other DJ services have DJs on call. They call a backup DJ who'll then bring backup equipment. Will your guests wait 45 minutes to an hour for the party to get up and running again? Probably not.

Then, I would say, "That's not going to happen with Steve Bender Entertainment." I turn the amp back on and say, "Why?" "Because we carry a backup amplifier, so if it goes out, we have the backup that flips on automatically, you're going to keep going, and every head in that crowd would go up and down. Every bride would look each other, 'Wow! That's different.'"

Now, backup is huge. That was back in the old days when a lot of guys didn't carry backup. Most people do now but what we did is we went a step further and we make sure that we reassure the couple of a couple of things.

That we arrive two hours prior to start time. They're not charged for that. That's our policy. Why two hours? DJ has on-call backup. If the back-up doesn't hear from him, back-up calls them and says, "Where are you?" If they don't talk to each other, backup's on their way automatically.

We have learned to provide a different level of service. Do we have to use the backup? Typically, no. In 40 years, we've had to use it one time but just that one little thing that you bring up can make a huge difference in the couple's mind of like, "Okay, these guys have us covered. They've got our back." I think, probably, those are some of the biggest concerns that they have that, also the fact that the DJ is experienced and knows how to handle an event.

Most brides have never put together a wedding so they're super nervous. The groom is sitting back and doing his own thing and showing up for the cake tasting and his job is to show up the day of the wedding. Whereas, the bride has all these stuff in front of her that she has to take care of and she has to act as if she's the expert.

I think she's looking for someone like us who's going to take her hand and say, "Look, we're going to walk you through this. We're going to give you sample timelines. We're going to explain to you how to put together a timeline. Then, on top of that, we're going to run the show for you so you're going to be able to sit back and relax and enjoy the day. You're not going to have to worry about, okay, it's time to do this, this, this and this."

You see a relief on the couple's face when you explain those things to them. They relax when they see you're stepping in and saying we're going to take care of you. We're going to take that off your shoulder. I think that's the stuff that they're looking to have alleviated in their minds, I guess.

What are some of the little known pitfalls or common mistakes that you've seen that couples make when they're trying to plan a successful wedding day that you'd like to make people aware of?

Over control where every minute detail is micro detailed. A good example would be a timeline where, a lot of times, the couples will focus so minutely on a timeline not realizing that the timeline, it's not going to go exactly on time. Yes, it says you're going to do the cake at 8:30 and, the fact of the matter is you do the cake at 8:45 or at 8:20 versus the exact 8:30. That's not the big deal.

What's the big deal is that the flow is proper and that it's flowing at the natural flow of what the event is. Like if you have a stream of water, if you dam it up and all of a sudden the water starts accumulating, and boom! You have a disaster because things aren't getting done when they should've and have that natural flow in regards to the event.

Another big misconception that couples have is surrounding the music selection for their wedding. They have a tendency to focus a little too intently on the music, thinking it's their job to put together a list and the DJ's job play the songs on that list.

That's typically not the best event. You're hiring professionals to do their job. Yes, the professional wants the input of the couple and, yes, we're going to play the songs that you want to hear that are the most important songs but focus is really, really important, allowing the entertainer to use all the tools that they know how to use. The songs are the tools to us. Being able to take those songs and interweave them with the songs that you want to make a successful night for not just for the bride and groom but for the guests and everybody who's there so that everybody, in one giant group, is unified into this really, really fun event.

Can you give us an example of how you helped a couple either overcome an obstacle like this or avoid a pitfall or create a really successful reception, something noteworthy?

Over the years, we'll have couples come in that are very adamant about their music. They'll say, "We don't want there to be any requests. We don't want there to be anything except what's on our list. This is our day. We want our music." Well, there's a couple of things you got to look at with that.

Number one, until you drill down and understand what they're saying, you can't really give them a determination. Good example would be this. You may have a couple that says, "You know, we want the songs that we want. We don't want people coming up requesting even if it's our mom or our dad and so forth.

In a DJ's mind, they may be thinking, "Boy, this is going to be a problem." Seriously, they could choose a lot of really bad stuff that nobody would want to dance to and you're not going to be able to use your tools. It's like going to the surgeon and asking them to take your appendix out but then telling the surgeon, "Oh, by the way, you can only use a spoon. You're not to use your normal tools and so forth."

Typically, I use that example with couples. I'll say, "Well, okay. We can do that. However, it's probably going to be painful and it may kill you but if that's what you want?" I mean, that's what you're basically doing in that situation. Once you drill down, you may say to yourself, "You know what, the list of songs that they want you to play are exactly what you would probably recommend anyway." In those situations, you go with it because you've drilled down, you understand what the couple wants.

I had another bride who literally told me, "I've danced at weddings of my friends and they played stupid songs, all the stuff that everybody likes and everybody was dancing ... Cupid shuffle ... We don't want any of that stuff."

I literally drilled down to find out what she wants. She goes, "I want songs that I want. This is my day." I explained to her, saying, "I understand that. At the same time, you have to realize that the couples or the other people may not have the same expectations of the music."

Mass appeal radio exists for a reason. Mass appeal anything exists for a reason. It's mass appeal. Everybody tends to have a broad appeal or are broad likening of what they expect. On the other side, you can color outside of the lines a bit. You can interweave it in but what I literally did was

I pulled up the top 200 most requested songs and I said, "Tell you what, let's go through this list. Out of this list, tell me which songs would be okay to play."

We went through that list and there were only three songs. That was it. I literally had to tell that bride, "I'm not sure we're going to be the best service for your event. Based upon what we do and where we've had our success and have our five-star ratings, we may not be the right service. You're looking for something a little bit more eclectic than what we do." She was actually shocked that I would say that.

It's funny because I recommended some other services to her. She went to other services and they basically told her the same thing. She wound up, eventually, just saying, "I'm just going to rent a little sound system and I'm going to play my iPod because that's what I want." Because none of the other companies, honestly, were willing to take on the business.

The other companies called me and asked, "Steve, did you talk to so and so? She said that you didn't want the business. Well, after we talked to her, we understood why."

They said, "Well, we think Steve was trying to help you."

I spoke to her in a very professional manner, I wasn't egotistical. I told her, "Look, my goal is for every client to be a raving lunatic fan of what we do. I want you to tell your boss when the boss says, 'We've got a Christmas party coming up or we've got a picnic or whatever, I want you to be able to confidently say, "These are the guys you need to call." I want, when you've got a friend getting married for you to say, "This is the person you need to call." We want to be that group of people to you because 50% of our business comes from referrals."

It makes no sense to take on a client that you know you're not going to be able to satisfy. I mean, that little bit of money you're going to make off that event versus the potential for a negative review and/or just whatever it may be, it's just not worth it. I'd rather have an open slot on a date like that.

I've learned that over the years. When was I first starting out years ago, you take the money that comes in and so forth but, I think, I've learned to try to protect myself and also my people from situations like that.

So you just made them aware of a problem that they potentially could face, is that right?

Yeah. Typically, where the problems will arise will be in their music. They'll give you a music list and the music list may not be that great. You can look at it and you can see, okay, this is a little bit different. That's where you drill down typically on, "Hey, tell me a little bit about the people that are going to be there. What's the age group that they're going to be? What are your expectations in terms of what you want for the night?"

Good example. They may say, "Well, you know, honestly, there's not going to be a lot of dancing at our event and we know that from past weddings that we've been to with our family."

In that case, this list that they gave you may be okay because their expectation is there's not going to be a lot of dancing. I can look at the list and know that there's not going to be a lot of dancing. However, there may be a situation where, in their mind, they're like, "No, we don't like line dances. We don't want any line dances at all. They're played at weddings all the time. You'll hear five or six of them. We don't want that throughout the night."

A lot of people don't realize this but the wedding reception is a thank you to the guest. If we want to simplify this, they're bringing the gift for your new marriage. They're getting the free meal out of it. They're getting whatever the expectation is. They want a fun, entertaining time. Their expectation of music is going to be different typically than the bride and groom.

The two of you, you're together, you have a lot of similarities. The other people, it's going to be a mass appeal audience. You're going to have 200 people. They're going to like different things so you have to do a little bit more mass appeal. What about this suggestion? Typically, the songs that you don't want are the songs that will get requested the most. It may not be a bad idea to look at this list of these five songs that you don't want and say, out of these five, this is the one that I can handle being able to hear.

Just giving us that one instrument, that one tool could potentially make a huge difference because it's a line dance that we can possibly use to get people on the floor, a large group of people from there.

We can use that song to build on the rest of the music you have here. We can throw this in, sandwich it between this, and go from there. Typically, you'll see the couple going, "Yeah, you know that does make sense."

I also bring up the fact that you have to realize, during the reception, it's going to be a whirlwind. You're not going to remember a lot of it sometimes. You're going to be going out sometimes and taking pictures with the photographer, doing ring shots, doing the sunset shots while the party's going on. Well, that's a great time when we can utilize maybe some things that will get the guests on the floor. They're like, "Well, you know what? That's a good idea. That's right."

We have to explain to the bride and the groom that they're going to be walking the tables. They maybe tell us, "We're not dancers. We're not really going to dance a lot." Well, if that's the case, you need to let us play the songs for the people who are dancers because you're giving me a list of songs for non-dancers.

I wouldn't think twist it or send it back to them but to say, "Look, okay, so you're telling me you're a non-dancing group and this is the music you like. You know what? That makes sense. You're more cerebral in terms of your musical taste, what you like, and so forth. That's great.

However, for the crowd that is a dancing crowd, these are the songs that are going to really hit the button, so maybe allow us to use some of these trigger songs that are going to help us while you're walking the tables, while you're doing all these other things where you're not really interested in dancing." Typically, you're able to turn it around with that, with things like that.

Steve, what inspired you personally to become a DJ entertainer and start Steve Bender Entertainment?

At 11 or 12 years old, I was just a little kid and I was a shy kid. It was just, I guess, a way for me to be different and I was also doing radio at that time. I got into a little, tiny radio station and it just seemed to make sense. Then, all of a sudden, I was making really, really good money instantly doing parties, school dances and private parties. That was like, "Wow!"

Then, I thought, "Boy, if I have some other people with me, I could make money by doing more dances," and that's what I did. Then, what happened was, totally by accident, we were the only game in town at that time. Then, what happened was these girls that we were doing high school dances with graduated and, all of a sudden, a few years later, they're getting married. We were the only DJs they knew. All of a sudden, we started learning how to do in, whatever, late 70s, early 80s, how to do weddings.

Now, all of a sudden, you know, there was a totally different market that I never even thought of, that I just fell into just as a natural progression. Then, the radio thing was really big because I was on the big, massive top 40, number one radio station in town and I wound up getting all the high schools in the area. Literally, in all Cincinnati, I was doing a lot of the business, and the teachers were getting married, the students were getting married when they graduated. I mean, literally, I built it by accident but, I think, also, we had a good quality product. I had really strong DJs and it was a totally different era and way of doing things.

Then, from there, we became a big deal and then we had only one real competitor. It was a company that started here in Cincinnati that eventually became a national chain. They're out of business now. They just went out probably about eight, ten years ago, maybe somewhere around there. They had a really bad reputation because that's the problem I see with DJ services is they start out, they do whatever, and they expand too quickly.

They started doing quantity rather than quality?

Yeah. Well, quantity's okay if you can control ... What they do is they expanded too much stuff. They start getting bigger and they start adding in all these other stuff and, all of a sudden, they lose focus on what they really are good at or what they can manage effectively. They start becoming more of a lighting company or more of a décor company or all of it all in one. They lose control of the product and they just start sending anything out there.

Can you share a lesson that you learned early on that still impacts how you perform today?

At the actual event, one of the things that I actually train my people to do is to, you know, respond to the client versus responding to your own ego. What I mean by that is, this has happened to everybody. You're coming out of a slow set and you're going to a fast set and you've got everybody packed on the floor and dad walks up and says, "Hey, my mom is 88 years old and she's getting ready to leave here. She wants to leave here in a few minutes or in a little bit. Could you play String of Pearls? That was her song, or Can't Help Falling In Love by Elvis," or whatever it may be. "That was her and my grandfather's song and she would so love to hear that song tonight."

A typical DJ response is going to be something like, "Yeah, you know what? I just got the crowd packed with people. I guess I'll get to that song here in just a bit. I'm going to stretch this out." Well, dad's going to typically say, "Okay, but she's going to be leaving here in just a little bit." He goes, "Oh, no problem. We'll get to it." The DJ will look at it from the standpoint of this is what is happening. I've got to keep the floor going. I don't want to lose this crowd. If I throw Can't Help Falling In Love, one, two songs after a slow set and I'm playing this, I'm going to lose this crowd. I can't rebuild it.

That is the exact opposite mindset, in my opinion, of what you need to have. My mindset is, number one, I know for a fact, because my dad's 88 years old, when dad or grandma says, "Hey, we want to leave." It doesn't mean in a few minutes. It means they're leaving now. They have a different schedule as they should have. They've earned it. They're going to be leaving now so when dad walks up to you and say, "Hey, can you play this song for my mom? She's getting ready to leave," you need to take action.

What I typically will do, the way you do it is you turn it into a moment. A good example of a moment would be, okay, you took something where, yeah, it's going to kill the floor but if you're a good DJ, you're going to rebuild it. Here's the thing that I do and that I train my people to do. You might say, "Hey, I've got something really special here tonight. We've got a young lady this evening who, her special song with her husband 56 years ago or whatever it was, was [name the song]... She would love for you to dance with her tonight and celebrate that memory with her this evening. What do you all say?" And you have grandma out there.

There's not one person on that dance floor that's not going to applaud, that's not going to dance with grandma, that's not going to stay on that floor even though you just interrupted Uptown Funk. You just turned it into a moment. Suddenly, you've got a photograph that's really special, that's a memory from that moment that everybody's going to remember, you've got dad who's super happy, okay, so your tip potential just went up. You've got all of these other stuff going on. You took a potential negative and turned it into a moment, a memory in a positive, right then and there. You know what? After that song, everybody's still on that floor cheering, you go right back into whatever you're doing. You're set and you look like a hero.

What's one thing that we may not have covered that you could share with a bride who's wanting a successful wedding?

Well, to hire the top professionals in whatever category it is, DJ, photographer, cakes, and give them the room to do what has earned them their five-star rating. Give them the ability to give you the service that has earned them their ratings through the years.

What that means is realizing that it's probably not going to be the best idea to 100% control every single element. You need to let the professionals who knows what they're doing do it and put the trust in those individuals to do it. That's probably the biggest thing that I'm hearing from a lot of different vendors.

Steve, how can someone find out more and connect with you?

We're real easy to find. I mean, number one, our website is www.stevebender.com. The internet is, number one, a great way. We're everywhere. We're on the Knot.com, we're on WeddingWire.com. We're highly recommended by venues and photographers and the top names in the industry.

We're pretty doggone easy to find simply because we've been around forever and we have a very strong reputation even amongst our competitors and I'm very upfront with all of my clients. I ask them when they're sitting down to talk to me, "Who else are you looking at?" They'll tell me typically. "Oh, we're looking at this guy or this other DJ." I literally will always give accolades to my competition and I'll say, "Oh, my gosh! You know, Randy, this company, he's outstanding. He's been doing it for so long, he and his wife own it. "

That's very different than what most companies do. Most companies are actually very, especially guys, very aggressive and will go a different route. I'll tell you what. I booked more events from just being upfront and honest and talking nicely about my competition than I ever would've being negative. It puts you in a different league.

How about a phone number folks can reach you?

Oh, yeah. 513-732-1963. We are a full-time service so we're in during normal business hours and evening appointments are always available, however Fridays, Saturdays, and Sundays are tougher because we are often in the field.

ERIC CHUDZIK

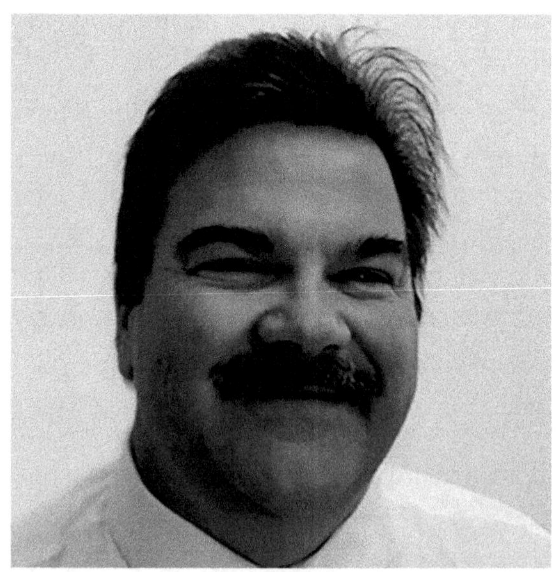

A Conversation with Eric Chudzik
of Electric Blue Entertainment

Eric tell us about your business and the types of clients you serve.

Well, my business is a DJ service and we deal primarily with weddings. We serve our brides and grooms, mostly brides and we are there to help them have a great wedding reception from beginning to end.

What do you feel are the biggest myths or misconceptions about the role the DJ plays in the success of a wedding?

Oh, that's a great question. What happens is, people think that you get your top 40 songs, or your best songs of all time, you bring the equipment, you press play and the party happens and nothing's further from the truth.

Basically, we're the go-to guy for everybody that day, the caterer, the photographer, everybody revolves around us. We talk to the bride and groom, we're kind of like their go-to person to say, "This is what we're going to do and when we're going to do it" and then everybody else kind of bounces off us.

"Oh, we're going to do that next. Oh, we're going to do that next." You could say, we're an unofficial wedding coordinator.

What are some common mistakes that you've seen made when couples try to plan a successful wedding reception that you'd like to make people aware of?

I'd like to make them aware of over doing things. In other words, they over budget time, so they'll say, "At 3:05, we're going to do this" and you want to have a loose schedule, but you've got to remember, it's a real life, real time unrehearsed day.

It's going to go off beautifully, but don't micromanage it to the point where you're crazy at like, "Oh, its 9:05, we need to do this now!" It just makes you crazy. Definitely don't do that and don't overdo the music either. A lot of people will give us a list that is longer in time than the actual day. Watch your list, do the songs that you really want and you'll have a fun day.

What are some of the most common fears brides have about working with a DJ like yourself?

I've had brides just panicking, they want that dance floor to be full. Their fear is the DJ playing a song and just nobody dancing. I feel that, that's my job. That's what we do. We get that dance floor full. We use the material, the songs, and the type of wedding that the bride and groom want... and then we turn that to the guest and we make that party happen, that reception jump.

It's not their job to make it jump, but it is their job to tell us what they want to make that party what it's going to be. So it turns out to be the music that they want, people dancing, and everybody has a great time.

Can you give us an example of one of the more interesting or challenging receptions that you've done and how you've helped the couple?

We had a few that were in remote areas and we really tried to help them out with electricity needs, with the type of locale, like they would have a wedding where the carriage would come up and it was down on a field, then I was on a porch of the house.

Then we went to the tent in another area for the reception and what I did was I brought two systems so that we can do a seamless flow from the ceremony music moving along to the reception where there's music all the time.

Terrific. Eric, what inspired you to become a wedding professional DJ entertainer specifically to begin with?

You know, it's funny. Nothing's changed in over 25 years. It seems like brides and grooms needed a friend. Somebody that will help them plan the wedding. The photographer takes care of his end. The meal will be there with the caterer or the venue, but who is going to put it all together and that's kind of what we've done from the very beginning.

We've always said, "Here is your day, from beginning to end and we're going to help fill that. You tell us what you want us to do and when." Once we have that itinerary, we follow it because we're professionals and we make your day just a lot of fun. Its stress free and a lot of fun for the bride and groom.

Can you share a lesson that you've learned early on that still impacts how you perform today?

Yes. We are very much about being prepared. We try not to have a one point of failure, in other words, we have back-up. Back-up people, back-up systems, back-up vehicles, back-up on the music in case, who knows what could happen? We always back-up so basically, the bride and groom don't have to worry about that, because we have that taken care of.

Most cases when we do the back-up thing, the bride and groom never know, because the wedding goes on flawlessly. Oh, and the other thing is, we're always early. Be early. We always try to be very early for brides and groom and for their weddings and wedding receptions.

What's one things that we may not have covered that you could share with a bride who's wanting to have a successful day?

Plan ahead with what you want. Dream about your day. Fill out those plans to have that day just perfect for you and don't stress out about it. Just set it and then forget it, which is kind of cliché, but basically, it's just like, have fun on that day.

Don't stress out and then we'll take care of what we need to take care of while you guys just have fun. In my 25 years of doing this, one thing I emphatically know is... if the bride and groom have fun on the day, guess what, everybody else seems to and it's usually a successful reception.

Terrific. How can someone learn more about you and your services and possibly connect with you and possibly hire you?

Okay, well I have an email address, it's very easy DJ@electricblueentertainment.com. We would love to hear from you. We definitely talk a lot before the wedding. It's not just like, “Here you go and this is what we do and we'll see you later.”

We're always in contact with our brides and grooms, “Hey, we have an idea for this, can you help us out?” We love to hear from them and help them out in any way we can.

RICK ADDY

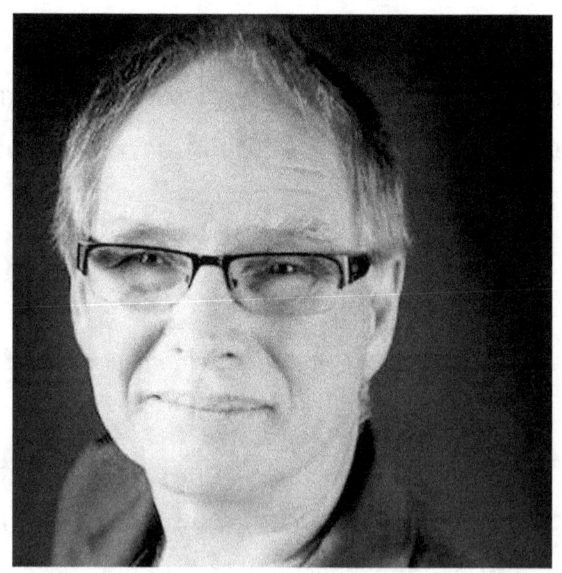

A Conversation with Rick Addy
of Pro MCDJ Entertainment

The excitement of an upcoming wedding can blind many couples to the extent of details required to have the reception music and dance far exceed their expectations. Having an experienced Professional DJ Entertainer guide them through the process is key to a great celebration says Rick Addy, owner of Pro MCDJ Ent. ....creating unforgettable, fun celebrations is what we learn about with Rick today

Q: Tell us about Pro MCDJ Ent and the clients you serve?

We're a professional mobile DJ service, providing a range of services from music and DJ to room decor lighting, audio visual, MC duties, and special effects along with reception planning. Our clients range in age from 20 to 60 years of age, getting married in the greater South Western Ontario area.

Q: What inspired you to become a professional DJ?

Through public and high school I had been involved in music and also loved to go dancing. So music was a huge part of my early years. Several years out of high school, I was approached to have a look at learning the DJ trade with a local company. After only 3 nights of training, I was thrust into service at a wedding and I've been hooked ever since. I loved entertaining people, seeing them dance, react to your music selections and have a great night.

Q: Can you share a lesson you learned early on that still impacts how you perform your service today?

There's been many along the way, but I would have to say the day I learned to seize a moment as it happens rather than waiting for a good time to fit a song in was huge. ex: Playing the "one" song before grandma leaves smack in the middle of a hot dance set so she can dance once or the kids song for the 3 nieces before they go home even though no one else will dance to it. It's a small thing but much appreciated and a great DJ can get their dance floor back in short order.

Q: What do you feel are the biggest myths or misconceptions about the role your service plays in the success of a wedding?

First off, I have to say there are more great DJ professionals in the industry than ever before who do great work. However, to this day the misconception that what we do is easy and we "just play music" is still the biggest. If there's one Achilles' heel to every great DJ is we make what we do look easy. People say anyone can play music, which today's technology makes possible quite easily. However, "just playing music" will kill a party faster than you can say Justin Bieber. :) It's the pre planning, the coordination with other vendors, strong organizational and observation skills, mic skills along with music mixing skills and timing that truly creates a great celebration.

You can find out more about us at:

www.professionalmc.com

www.facebook.com/ProMCDJEnt

519-851-8749

GEORGE PENN

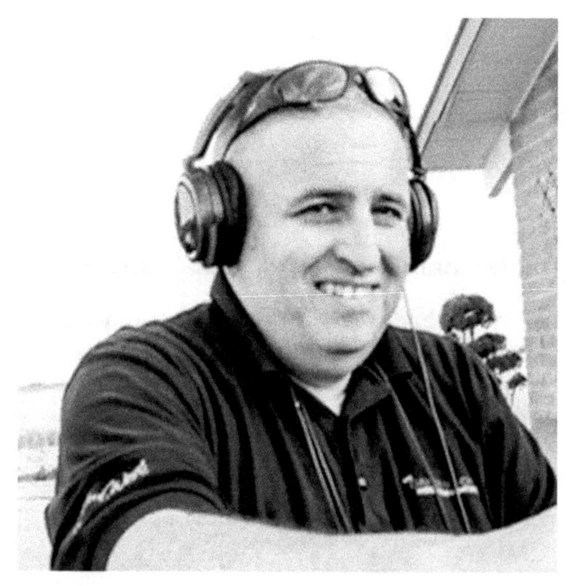

A Conversation with George Penn
of XPROi - The Dance Machine

George, tell us about your business and the types of clients you serve.

I operate a disc jockey company and we service wedding clients in central Washington as well as Northeast Oregon.

What do you feel are the biggest myths or misconceptions about the whole that you play as a DJ in the success of wedding?

The biggest misconception in my mind, is that all we do is play music. That we are just a human jukebox. We are so much more than that.

We help them with planning their event, we help them with day-of coordination, and definitely playing music is part of what we do, but it's not the mindless work that so many people think. It's not like we are a human iPod or that human jukebox I talked about.

A lot of time and effort goes into making the perfect music mix. Advance planning, talking with the brides and grooms to figure out what's going to make the party kick, what's going to get people up and out of their seats so we can help them make memories. It's not just listening to music. It's so we can get people interacting and having fun. That's what we do to overcome the misconceptions.

What are some of the most common fears that brides and grooms have about having a successful wedding day working with the DJ like yourself?

Some of the biggest fears that the brides and grooms have, a lot of times, their fear is based on what they've heard from others, such as the DJ may not show up to their event. That's one of their biggest fears, if that makes sense.

Another fear, and I see this one quite a lot from brides and grooms is, they're afraid that nobody's going to dance, or that we are going to play the wrong music. While having such concerns are totally understandable, they never, in my many years in this business, have come to fruition.

Through prior planning we make sure that we are hitting the vibe that they want us to. If it's going to be a country wedding, we are going to have the best, hottest country dance songs that their crowd, their people, are going to dance to. If it's top 40, same thing.

We go through and we do the research in advance to make sure that the atmosphere and good vibes they want for their guest is what they get.

What are some of the pitfalls or common mistakes that you see couples make when trying to plan a successful wedding?

One of the biggest mistakes that people make is they allow the party to get spread out throughout the venue. There was one occasion where we were doing an event at a casino and nightclub on a Sunday night where there was nothing going on there.

The bride and groom decided that they wanted to play the role of dealers at the casino... tuxedo, wedding dress and deal cards to their people. That drew everybody away from what we were doing in (the reception) and everybody disappeared for a good 45 minutes. Once they finished dealing the cards, around half the people returned, while the other half left.

In a room where the main party is taking place, that's mission-critical. I don't know how many times I've seen it where, if we are doing an outdoor wedding at a farm or something like that, people will disperse from the main party area and it just gets diluted.

It just doesn't go down well to pull people away and is something brides and grooms should keep in mind when planning their big day. Things like photographers dragging the bride and groom way and keeping them away from the party for an hour is something to think about. The brides and groom's absence is a sure turn off for their guests, giving them valid reasons to leave when it happens.

Can you give an example of one of the biggest challenges you might have faced while performing a wedding and how you helped a couple overcome a challenge or a problem?

This was an odd ball. We were DJ'ing an event on the Columbia River at a very nice house. The house was expensive. The bridesmaids somehow found a stash of bottle rockets and were lighting them off before the ceremony. Nobody thought anything of it.

Halfway through the ceremony, as the bride and groom were walking down the aisle, we look over and the house is on fire. We were to. What do you do?

We had to stop the ceremony and put out the fire before we could continue, because we didn't want the property owner to lose a million-dollar home because of some bridesmaids being stupid. That's the most off-the-wall off the hook story that I have for my 32 year career of doing this. During less turbulent times, we help clients every day with all sorts of challenges such as music selection and their planning.

George, what did inspire you to become a DJ?

Now that's an interesting story. Going back to my schooldays and when I'd just graduated from high school, my school had a closed door policy, which basically meant that if you weren't a student there, you couldn't go to the dances.

This was somewhat of a dilemma for me because even though I had graduated, several of my friends were still at the same school. I wanted to somehow be involved with the dances.

That's where, out of necessity if you will, I came up with the idea to buy some equipment and learn to be a DJ so I could still be at the dances and be with my friends. That's initially what got me started. A couple of years thereafter, and having my first full set of equipment, I realized that I really loved doing everything surrounding the activities of being a DJ and in 1985 started doing weddings for close friends and family. Things kind of snowballed to where I am today. Taking into account the wedding I did last weekend, my total is 1307 events!

It has been a lot of fun and I still look forward to doing weddings every weekend. I still get the butterflies and a little anxious before the show as I want things to be perfect for the couple. I want them to have the absolute best time of their lives on their wedding day and I give everything I've got to ensure that happens.

Can you share a lesson that you learned early on that impacted how you performed today?

Yes I do. It sounds simplistic, but so important. The lesson I always keep in mind is, it's not my day. It's the couple stand. More importantly, one of my company slogans is, *"Even when it's not about the bride, it's still all about the bride."* It's their special day and importantly it's her special day. It's the day she's been planning since she was in kindergarten or first grade. Having to realize that it's not about me and it's all about them is the biggest lesson I learned early on and as a company, we carry that through to this day. It's so not about us.

What's one thing that we made of covered then you could share with someone is wanting a successful wedding?

That's a tough one. The price issue. You get what you pay for and that's cliché. Planning is important. Taking the time to work with your vendors, not just myself, the DJ, but all the other vendors that are associated with the day will help the day go so much smoother.

In the DJ scenario, getting your information back in a timely manner that helps us be more prepared to help the wedding customer. It's the same with every wedding vendor. Be it a photographer, photo booth operator, or caterer.

Communication is key and communicating as often as possible. Even more important key is getting and keeping the line of communication open from early on and keeping them going through the end of the evening.

How can someone find out more and connect?

We're very easy to find at www.xproi.com and Facebook https://www.facebook.com/TheDanceMachineTC. We are always available by phone: 509-628-5288 is the office number.

DAVE PETRY

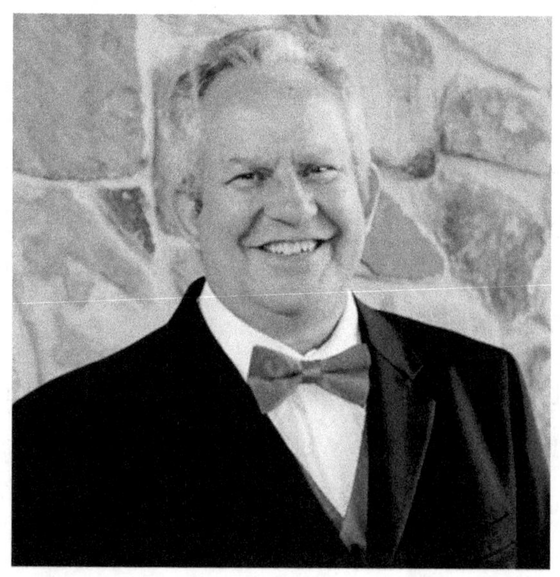

A Conversation with Dave Petry
of DJ Dave Productions

We're heading over to Houston, Texas to meet a one of a kind wedding specialist. Their company is so in demand, they'll perform for over three hundred and fifty weddings this year alone, can you believe that?

DJ Dave Productions provides personalized DJ services that reflect their clients' individual style. They provide dazzling light shows to set the mood and photo booths to capture your magic moments.

Founded eight years ago, they've won awards such as the Best of the Knot Best of Weddings and the Couple's Choice Award from Wedding Wire for the last four consecutive years.

David Petry was also co-author on a book named the Ultimate Wedding Reception.

What makes you different from all of your competition?

DJ Dave Petry: Well first off and foremost I would say that the attention to detail and the personalized service, customer service, what we provide to each of our individual clients' needs. We focus primarily on the bride and the wedding industry. We want to understand exactly what the brides' needs are, what she wants, understand her vision and then we actually build our entertainment package around that.

Mark Imperial:You know brides have so many choices today. How do you specifically continue to build your business and grow faster than any other company around?

DJ Dave Petry: That's a great question, Mark. There are several factors and I'll try to highlight them as well as I can. First and foremost, I would say that we are very, very active on a daily basis.

My number one priority is that we're responsive and timely in our response to any inquiry, any communication that we have with our clients because as we all know clients have a need, they need to be supported to make sure that we understand everything they're looking for and whenever they have a question we need to be responsive. So if we get an inquiry, we always try to turn that around within the thirty minutes to make sure that we do respond to it.

We also network a lot. We participate in all the major wedding shows in our Houston market, which are incredible shows. Many open houses, we work, we spend a lot of time in our community with all the venues and our vendor colleagues I would say is very strong part of what helps us grow our business faster than anyone else.

Mark Imperial:Now I know your services are really unique. How do brides find you and how do you know when you're really a good match for each other?

DJ Dave Petry: It's amazing the way that we've built our marketing system is that many of our clients when they reach us and they find us, they've already qualified us as a potential candidate that they want to do business with, but how they find us is by several means.

By the website. We have a remarkable website presence, it's very intuitive, it's very helpful, and our clients can look in there. They can see our reviews. They can look at our all the services we have to offer. It's very easy.

Our clients also have access to our social media presence where they can find us on Facebook, Twitter and Pinterest. Those are the usual ways in which we can be found.

Mark Imperial:Now what's the most important thing that you do on a daily basis to serve your clients and grow your business?

DJ Dave Petry: On a daily basis, we don't stop until we finish the task at hand for that day. That's one of my main mantras to make sure that nothing is left on the desk, no question has not been answered for our brides.

Being timely, as I mentioned before that's our main goal. Reaching out, spending time in the community with all the different networking meetings, all the different trade groups. We're probably visiting fifteen to twenty brides a week with initial meetings and our finalization meetings to make sure we understand what they're looking for. We support our local community too so everybody really knows who we are and where we're at.

Mark Imperial:Right on. What would you say is the number one thing a bride should consider for having a successful wedding celebration?

DJ Dave Petry: First of all I would recommend the bride to do their homework and do their research and today's bride is very smart and they are doing their research. Check out the reviews of the DJ's that you're wanting to interview because past success leaves clues, past performance is a good indicator of future performance as well.

The brides also need to make sure that their entertainment company they're looking at is locked into their vision and absolutely on the same page. We want to implement the key elements to personalize entertainment to our brides and grooms on their special day. It's almost like being a part of their family when it's all said and done. If their DJ company, or their entertainment is not on the same page, the reception will be less than spectacular.

Mark Imperial: Ah. ***How do brides find out more from you?***

DJ Dave Petry: Well first off you can find us on the website. Website is www.djdaveproductions.com and or call us at 713-806-1085.

Mark Imperial:Dave, you're truly rocking it out. Three hundred and fifty weddings this year alone?

DJ Dave Petry: Yes sir.

Mark Imperial:I can't even imagine being as popular as you and managing all that and maintaining that stellar reputation you must be totally rocking it out so congratulations Dave. I wish you continued success.

DJ Dave Petry: Well thank you very much Mark. I appreciate being on your show.

KOKO BROTHERS

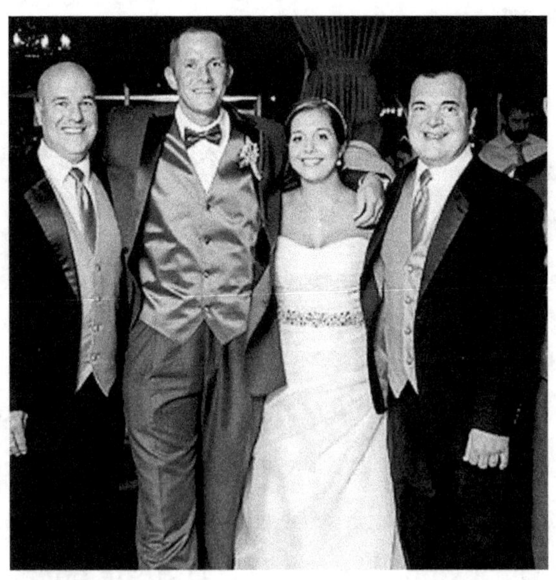

A Conversation with Lou & Angelo Koko
of Koko Brothers Entertainment

Tell us about Koko Brothers Entertainment and the type of clients that you serve?

Lou Koko: Have you ever gone to a wedding where the music was just perfect, the dance floor packed and the vibe and lighting were just right and everyone had an amazing time? Yeah, that's what we do for our clients every weekend.

Angelo Koko: Koko Brothers entertainment is the unique DJ and MC team of Lou and Angelo Kokkinakos. Koko Brothers provides unparalleled wedding day entertainment for clients that are looking for the perfect balance of fun and elegance. Our two person DJ and MC team offers a level of service that wedding clients deserve for such a momentous occasion. Weddings are all about timing.

With our two person team, we are able to constantly entertain your guests while never dropping the ball on communicating with all your vendors. This simple approach, which vendors and our clients love, is the key to successful and stress free weddings. Yes, we really are brothers and the way we see is, it's all about family. Our family taking care of your family.

What do you feel are the biggest myths or misconceptions about the entertainment as it relates to the success of a wedding?

Lou Koko: I think the biggest one is any DJ can DJ a wedding. It just takes a different mindset, a different mentality than doing a club or doing a Mitzvah or doing any other type of party. The language that you use, the way you talk to people. You're not necessarily going to talk the same way in a nightclub than you're going to talk at a wedding reception. I strongly believe that the misconception that any DJ can do a wedding is a fallacy.

Angelo Koko: I think one of my most thought about misconceptions when it comes to weddings is the DJ is really only about the music. With all these years of experience in doing weddings, the music is what gets the crowd going, it's what creates the energy, it's what creates the fun and excitement, but the reality is it's really about the planning. The timeline of everything.

Making sure that you're meeting with your clients in advance and going over all the details, all their wishes and all the preparation that goes into the front side to make sure that you're delivering exactly what they want on their wedding day. If you're just focused on the music, you're really not seeing the big picture. It's not about the music alone. The music being executed properly to the clients wishes.

Lou Koko: With that being said, talking about music, another misconception is that any DJ can play the music. You have to have a strong music programming knowledge. I know technology has made it easier now, but you still have to have a very strong basis of music programming.

Angelo Koko: Another common misconception is hiring a DJ comes down to the price and that DJs are all the same. That's one that really sits near and dear to my heart because I will probably say a dozen times to our clients any given day, it really comes down to that personality match. You can get a car for your wedding day, your limousine.

Ford is a great car company, but odds are on your wedding day, you're going to spend a little bit more and get Ford's higher end, and get a Lincoln stretch that day instead of a Ford. So it doesn't really come down to price. It's really going to be that right match that aligns you with a person that you trust on your wedding day to handle all your music, all your entertainment needs, MC'ing and of course the coordination of other vendors.

What are some of the most common fears that your clients have when it comes to working with a DJ Entertainer for their reception?

Lou Koko: A level of professionalism. Will they show up? How is their personality? Are they tacky? Will the DJ be prepared? Will the equipment be adequate? How do they dress? Will they address the crowd in a professional manner?

Angelo Koko: Of course a lot of fears that our clients have when they first look for a DJ is "will people dance?" People want to have a good time at their wedding and it's all about meeting with your entertainment options and discussing it and making sure, like Lou said, that there's a level of professionalism there. That they understand that we are committed professionals that are dedicated to show up, and deliver exactly what they're looking for. Again, so they know that they're not hiring a tacky DJ, they're not hiring a DJ that's going to be too stiff. They're hiring the person that matches their personality.

How do you recommend they find that out from you?

Angelo Koko: The best way for us to really inform our clients is to sit down together, meet and really just have an open dialogue on what their desires are for their wedding day, what their vision is and to really explain how our 20 plus years or experience have guided countless happy couples to excellent wedding receptions. Just really getting an understanding of what their needs are and just really making sure we're a good match for one another.

What are some of the little known pitfalls or common mistakes that people make when they're trying to plan a successful wedding day that you'd like to make people aware of?

Lou Koko: Hiring a friend or inexperienced vendor.

Angelo Koko: We dissect weddings endlessly, and we've learned that over the years, layout (of the room) is one of the key determining factors of a wedding reception. I know it sounds a little strange to say that, but we've been in some venues where the rooms are very segmented.

For example, a bar is down the hallway to the right, quite a bit of walk. Sometimes tables are set up in front of the DJ for guest to sit at. The dance floor is set up across the room. A lot of these factors will actually make the room very segmented and not very conducive to a nice, warm welcoming event where it's conducive to getting guests engaged and on the dance floor. In a perfect world, we don't want guest tables set up right in front of the DJ, we want the dance floor to be as close to us as possible. Just many factors like that that play into the whole entire success of the reception.

For example, room lighting. We don't want a room to be extremely bright. Again, back to the layout, if the room can't be dimmed down, great, we'll dim it down by means of just turning off the house lights and uplighting a room to give it the right feel and make sure it's highlighting things like columns in the room that are beautiful or different features of the room that add that warmth and that perfect atmosphere for your wedding reception.

Could you give us an example, how you've been able to help your couples achieve a successful reception?

Lou Koko: The way that we feel that really helps couples achieve a successful reception is the two person approach that we have done for many years after doing weddings on our own. We truly feel that the two person DJ and MC team offer the ultimate level of service. To do a wedding successfully, it requires us to be in two places at one time. This allows us to have more efficient communication with the vendors, the clients, the guests and the venue. We're guilty of always showing up extra early to each and every event. We love to utilize that time after we're set up and all dressed up as a last opportunity to make sure all the vendors are on board with the timeline, so we go over all the details and make sure that everyone is prepared for the event.

Angelo Koko: Another way we help our couples achieve success is just to call upon our 20 years plus of experience. We've performed at countless weddings over the years. After every wedding, we always treat it as a case study in and of itself. Understanding what we did, what really worked well, and what could we do a little different in the future to improve upon results.

It's a common thing around here, we say it all the time to our clients, and we're not trying to become a burger joint by any stretch of the imagination, but we always say to our clients, "there's no right way or wrong way. It's your way." We're really that open to our clients and really try to fulfill their wishes and desires. We also won't guide them to a foolish idea if experience has shown us something hasn't worked in the past.

We will definitely work with them and try to make sure that what they want to do is very logical, and that it would create a good outcome. Again, with over 20 years of experience and so many client referrals over the year, our track record has been that we really help deliver results that achieve success and great memories.

What inspired you to become wedding professionals?

Lou Koko: From a young age, I was very passionate about music. I remember the first record I got. My dad took me to get not one Elvis album, but six Elvis albums that were my very first records that I ever purchased. My father took me to get that and I remember that vividly. Music just became my passion. In college I started working in radio and DJ'ing in nightclubs.

While sharing my passion for music, I was approached by many people asking if I would DJ their wedding. After the first wedding, I realized my "office" had the coolest view in the world. While working, I watched couples' emotional first dance, parents' dances and people going crazy on the dance floor. It just became my passion to continue to pursue weddings and do this full time.

Angelo Koko: Like Lou, I loved music at an early age. I really got into the technology side of it. I played keyboard, and synthesizers were just the coolest thing to me. The whole entire 80s electronic music thing just made me really love music. So when Lou got into DJ'ing, I quickly embraced the audio and lighting technology of it all. That was just kind of my thing, the technology. I thought it was so cool how you could push the boundaries with technology and make things really unique and different and customized to your desire.

While going through college, I did some lighting in the theater program there. That led to us even getting more into the production realm beyond the DJ company, where we got the luxury of doing lighting for numerous concerts, and we still do many to this day.

That technology all came together and tied itself into what my vision was ultimately when I got married and realized, whoa, you can actually take a wedding reception and use all this cool audio, video and lighting technology that we've been using on concerts -- and transform a ballroom into this beautiful, elegant and most importantly – a unique room for your wedding reception to be held that's unlike what anybody else has done in that space, because you've customized it with all this beautiful technology.

Will you share a lesson or two you've learned early on that still impacts how you perform your service today?

Angelo Koko: One of the lessons I learned very early on was being a wedding DJ, like Lou said, often requires you to be in two places at once. There was a wedding we did several years ago and Lou did his usual thing in going around letting the vendors know that we're going to be doing the bouquet toss in about five minutes. He ran over to the bride, informed her of what was going on. He comes back to me, and everybody's smiling. Thirty seconds later, the bride beelines from across the dance floor straight over to us with this stressed look on her face. We knew right away before she was even within twenty feet of us that we had to make this bride happy again. She was not happy at that moment. She had learned in the several seconds after Lou left her that the florist did not deliver the throw away bouquet.

Lou quickly grabs her, gives her a glass of wine, says, "Don't worry about it, we're going to be ready in just a few moments. Assures her everything was going to be fine. While I stayed there entertaining the guests on the dance floor playing music, Lou actually ran out into the hotel lobby and gathered up some flowers, somehow managed to find a piece of ribbon and within minutes, made a throw away bouquet that nobody knew wasn't the throw away bouquet. Handed it off to the bride, bride is smiling from ear to ear, just loving it and everything went off without a hitch.

Lou Koko: You'd better believe from that lesson, we always check to see if the throw away bouquet is always there.

A lesson that we learned early on is you have only one chance to get it right. This is someone's big day. You've got to get it right on the first go, which takes us to an event that we did many years ago, where, within 45 minutes of the event, the power goes out in the whole entire building. So there's no electricity for the kitchen, there's no electricity for music, there's no lights in the room, it's just a blackout.

So Angelo right away looks at me and says, "I'm outta here." Doing what I can do to keep people entertained, Angelo runs to the closest Home Depot and rents a generator and is back within 25 minutes. He gets this generator up and going, we have music again. The kitchen even had some power and that's just one of those things that you learn that you have to plan out every single detail because incidents like this can happen.

Angelo Koko: Another thing that we learned very early on is communication with other vendors is absolutely key. We've seen it so many times that just giving a photographer, for example, a five minute heads up on something like a cake cutting can make all the difference to them. It gives them an opportunity to maybe change out a memory card, switch lenses or a battery pack. It just keeps everybody flowing and really in tune with one another. There's been times where, again, cake cutting for example, catering may not have the cake knives out on the table yet. You give them a five minute heads up. It really works well in the way we approach things because I'll make sure that I'm taking care of the music, Lou has the freedom to run around and just convey the important messages. It really comes down to communication.

What's one thing that we may not have covered that you could share with someone who is wanting a successful wedding day?

Angelo Koko: My one thing that we have not covered, and I would tell every client that's looking for any entertainment for their wedding reception would be to absolutely invest the time to meet with your DJ before making a decision. I feel that the key is that there's got to be the personality match there, that you have to be able to trust the person that you're working with.

Get to really spend time with them. The internet's a great tool because it gives information quickly but it lacks personality. DJ is all about personality. If you're going to have somebody speaking at your wedding reception, you want it to be in your voice. You want it to be in line with what you envision for your level of elegance, fun and flair for that day. Make sure that you take the time to get to know your DJ and just really spend time understanding what they truly offer and what really makes them separate, unique and different.

How can someone find out more and connect with you?

Lou Koko: In the age of instant online info, you can find anything in seconds, the only thing you can't find is personality. We feel so strongly that you need to meet with your DJ, that we have a very unique offer. Schedule a no obligation wedding day entertainment consultation with us and we will reward you for your investment.

A one hour meeting will not only educate you immensely about the role of your wedding DJ and MC, but should we not be the right match for you, we'll give you a $50.00 dining gift certificate for a great date night. Request your meeting today by emailing us: info@kokobros.com or call 410-666-8586.

ABOUT THE AUTHOR

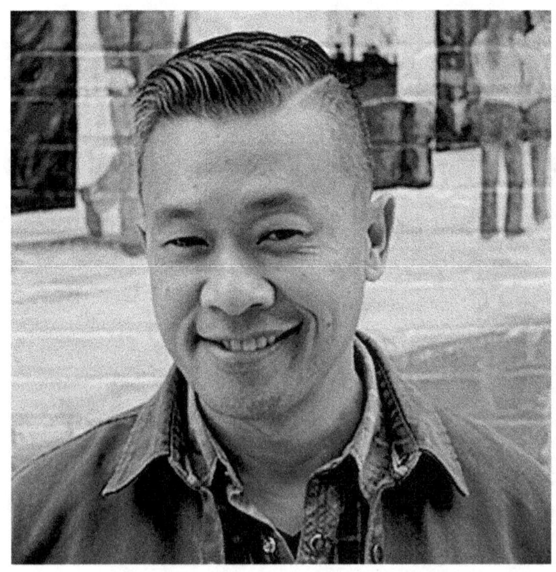

Mark Imperial is a Best Selling Author, Syndicated Business Columnist, Syndicated Radio Host, and internationally recognized Stage, Screen, and Radio Host of numerous business shows spotlighting leading experts, entrepreneurs, and business celebrities.

His passion is discovering noteworthy business owners, professionals, experts, and leaders who do great work, and sharing their stories and secrets to their success with the world on his syndicated radio program titled "Remarkable Radio".

Mark is also the media marketing strategist and voice for some of the world's most famous brands. You can hear his voice over the airwaves weekly on Chicago radio and worldwide on iHeart Radio.

Mark is a Karate black belt, teaches kickboxing, loves Thai food, House Music, and his favorite TV show is infomercials.

Learn more:

www.MarkImperial.com
www.ImperialAction.com
www.RemarkableRadioShow.com

www.ingramcontent.com/pod-product-compliance
Lightning Source LLC
LaVergne TN
LVHW020714110826
845149LV00012B/2255

9780998708508